EDWARD THE FIRST

BY

PROFESSOR T. F. TOUT

CHAPTER I

EARLY YEARS
1239-1258

EDWARD I. was born at Westminster on 17th June 1239. He was the first offspring of the marriage of Henry III. with Eleanor of Provence. Henry had long held in special reverence King Edward the Confessor, whose pious, weak, but amiable character in some ways is suggestive of his own. He therefore at once bade the child be called Edward, in memory of the holy king whose ashes reposed in the neighbouring abbey of St. Peter's. A papal legate performed the baptismal ceremony, and among the sponsors was the great Simon of Montfort, Earl of Leicester, newly reconciled to his royal brother-in-law after his audacious marriage with the widowed Countess Eleanor of Pembroke, King Henry's sister. Exceptional rejoicings attended the birth of the heir to the crown, for many feared that the young Queen was barren, and all were glad that a man-child, born on English soil and bearing an English name, had come into the world to settle the question of the succession to the throne. Significantly passing over the long line of foreign rulers who had borne sway in England since the Norman Conquest, an English chronicler gleefully traced back young Edward's genealogy to Alfred, the greatest of the old English kings. The laws of the good King Edward, after whom the child had been named, had been

1

the rallying cry of more than one generation of oppressed and down-trodden Englishmen. It was hoped that a new King Edward might renew the golden age of the holy Confessor. Groaning under weak and irresolute rule, wounded in all their dearest national aspirations. Englishmen looked forward from the dull present to the possibilities of a happier and brighter future. Nor were such hopes doomed to the disappointment which so commonly waits upon those who reckon upon the goodwill of princes. The son of the weak Henry and the greedy and unpopular Eleanor was destined to become the greatest of English monarchs.

Henry III. in many ways reminds us of Charles I. There is in both kings the same strict religious principle, the same high standard of private life, the same strong and pure domestic affections, the same intelligent, artistic temperament, the same graciousness, refinement, and love of culture. But a complete paralysis of will, an utter absence of straightforwardness, manliness, resolution, and clearness of vision, made Henry even more unfitted than Charles to act as ruler of England. Like Charles, Henry could never see that the times were changing. He held ideas of his own rights that the sons of the men who had wrested the Great Charter from King John could never allow to pass unquestioned. But it was not the policy so much as the want of policy of Henry that gave his subjects most offence. Thirteenth-century England had no objection to a strong king, who, clearly grasping the identity of interest between himself and his people, strove with might and main to grapple with anarchy and lawlessness, and drive the people into the

2

ways of sound rule and good order. Henry III. was too feeble, too frivolous, too idle, to be such a king. Moreover, he was jealous and suspicious of all able men. He was afraid to allow his ministers to exercise the powers that he was too weak to use himself. He strove to rule personally through clerks, dependents, and foreign favourites. The result was an almost complete collapse of all sound rule. While the material and spiritual activities of the nation were alike rapidly expanding, the strong centralised government which Henry II. had handed down to his sons was smitten with palsy. The begging friars were working out a great religious revival. The young enthusiasm of the Oxford masters had made England the home of an intellectual activity that could only be paralleled in the great University of Paris. Roger Bacon was preparing the way for English medicine and science. Vast and noble minsters in the new Pointed style were arising throughout the land, and proclaiming the culmination of mediaeval art. The English tongue was again becoming a vehicle for original literature, while in the learned Latin and the noble French a vigorous and abundant crop of great works were written by Englishmen. Englishmen were again conscious of national life and national unity. But with the weak Henry on the throne political progress that should match the rapid movement of the greatest and most constructive period of the Middle Ages could only be obtained through revolution.

Henry III. was himself in full sympathy with at least the religious and artistic movements of his time. His love of English saints, his anxiety to uphold English power abroad, shows that he was no mere

3

foreigner, as has so often been said. But his wife and his mother, a Provençal and a Poitevin, exercised an unhappy influence upon him. The Provençal and Savoyard uncles of his wife, his Poitevin half-brothers by his mother's second marriage, claimed the chief places in his court and councils, and aspired to the greatest offices, estates, and dignities in the land. Henry's superstitious fear of papal authority, combined with a shrewd sense of the temporal benefits to be got from close friendship with the spiritual head of the Church, exposed England to the invasion of a swarm of greedy foreign ecclesiastics. The very good points of Henry told against his popularity as a king. His appreciation of the great position of the Roman Church, his sympathy for the great wave of religion and culture which radiated from the France of St. Louis, and exercised an influence over western Europe only second to that exercised by the France of Rousseau and Voltaire, led Henry to a love of foreign manners and methods that became increasingly repugnant to his nobles. The barons of England might talk French at home, and vie with Henry in their love of French ways, but French-speaking Englishmen of the thirteenth century were no more good Frenchmen in the political sense than the French-speaking Vaudois or Genevese of to-day. Since the loss of Normandy under John, most of the English barons had become sound English patriots and enemies of French political influence, however fully they shared in the international civilisation of the French-speaking world.

Queen Eleanor of Provence exercised over Henry III. the same fatal influence that Henrietta Maria wielded over Charles I. She was indeed

4

a stronger and less frivolous character than her antitype. She inherited the subtle will and the bright poetic nature of her father, Raymond Berenger IV., the last Count of Provence of the native line, and himself not the meanest of the poets in the soft and melodious Provençal tongue. From her mother, Beatrice of Savoy, came the harder, clearer, more grasping temperament which was already a characteristic of the rising house of Savoy. She was one of four fair sisters, who all in their turn became queens.

> "Quattro figlie ebbe, e ciascuna regina,
> Ramondo Beringhieri."

Eleanor's elder sister Margaret was the wife of Louis IX., better known as St. Louis, then at the height of his power, and the strongest king who had ever as yet reigned in France. Her next sister, Sanchia, married Henry III.'s only brother, Earl Richard of Cornwall; while her youngest sister took the rich inheritance of Provence to her husband, Charles of Anjou, the brother of Louis IX. and the future conqueror of Sicily. But despite her French connections by marriage, Eleanor cannot herself be described as French in any strict sense of the word. Her family had long headed the unavailing struggle against the extension of North French influence into Languedoc and Provence. But a foreign girl from the south who never understood the ways and manners of Englishmen, and was, moreover, proud, greedy, extravagant, and overbearing, could not but exercise an evil influence over her weak, irresolute, and uxorious husband.

5

With all their faults, Henry and Eleanor were devoted to each other, and set an example of family life that was rare in those days of brutality and violence. They showed no less devotion to their children, and all through his life Edward was bound by the strongest ties of duty and affection to his kindly, affectionate, and loving father, and his proud, high-spirited, and passionate mother. Henry and Eleanor kept their son more about them than was usual in the formal households of the time. Up to the age of seven Edward was mainly brought up at Windsor under the care of Hugh Giffard. He seems to have been delicate, and to have suffered some severe illnesses. When he was seven he fell sick at Beaulieu Abbey, whither he had been taken by his mother to be present at the dedication of the church. For three weeks he lay in danger, and his mother, to the scandal of the strict Cistercians, insisted on staying in the convent that she might nurse him. A year later Edward was dangerously ill in London, and, at the King's request, prayers were offered up for his recovery in all the monasteries in and near the city. But as he grew older Edward got over his childish weakness. He became a tall, active, handsome boy, with bright flaxen locks, and proud, rather domineering manners. Nor was his education neglected. French, Latin, and English he could understand with equal facility, and, despite a stammer, he became ultimately an eloquent speaker in at least French and English. There is little evidence of his literary attainments and scanty proof of any love of books. Probably he was all through his life fonder of action than of speculation. But he certainly must have gone through that elaborate drilling in the routine of business which he afterwards strove in vain to enforce on his unhappy son. We are still more certain that he went through a careful legal training, perhaps under the guidance of the chancery clerk, Robert Burnell, who became his chaplain and confidential servant and to whom he was ever warmly attached. His father's real religious feeling ensured for Edward a strict religious education. The home lessons of purity and piety took a deep root, and all through his life Edward was honourably distinguished by the uprightness of his private life and the strength and fervour of his religious principles. Nor were the martial exercises which became a prince neglected. From an early age Edward became famous throughout Christendom as the bravest and most dexterous of warriors. He gained many notable successes in tournaments against some of the doughtiest champions of the day. He was equally expert in hawking and hunting, a fearless and dexterous horseman, and a proficient in all martial and manly sports, especially those that had in them a spice of danger. Among his most ordinary companions were his cousin, Henry of Almaine, the son of Richard, Earl of Cornwall, who was soon to become the titular king of the Romans, and his other cousins, the four young Montforts, of whom the eldest, Henry de Montfort, was nearly his own age. The Montforts were fierce, violent, brutal youths, and marked out for stormy and ill-fated careers. Not less violent were Edward's young Poitevin uncles, the Lusignans, the offspring of his father's mother, Isabella of Angoulême, by her second marriage with the Count of La Marche, and who came, like the Savoyard kinsfolk of Henry's wife, to share the bounty of their half-brother the King. Edward himself was not unmarked by the same taint in early manhood. After he had been given a household of his own, the violence and brutality of his followers involved their master in an unpopularity which was not quite undeserved. With lordly good nature, Edward bestowed his confidence on ruffianly officials, who oppressed and robbed his tenants in his name. Nor were his own acts blameless. Strange tales were told of the lawless deeds wrought by the heir to the throne out of mere love of mischief or wanton cruelty. The progresses of the Lord Edward with his band of 200 horsemen, mostly foreigners, were like the movements of a desolating plague. Not even Louis of France, the invader of England in King Henry's youth, had taken about with him such a band of ruffians and desperadoes. No common man had any rights that such high-spirited gentlemen could regard as sacred. They stole the horses, the waggons, and the provisions that came nearest to their hands. Even monks were spoiled and maltreated by these reckless youths. One day, when Edward paid a visit to his uncle Richard at Wallingford, his followers took violent possession of the neighbouring priory, and, driving out and insulting the lawful owners, stole their food, destroyed their property, and beat their servants. On another occasion Edward was passing along a road, and, out of mere wantonness, ordered his followers to cut off an ear and pluck out an eye of a harmless youth who had happened to cross his path. The most gloomy forebodings were expressed as to what would happen under so headstrong and reckless a ruler. But if courtly complacency is wont to magnify the virtues of young princes, common gossip is at least as apt to exaggerate their vices. Regard for human suffering was a very rare quality in the Middle Ages, at least outside church and cloister. Yet it is hard to believe that Edward was guilty of anything worse than youthful carelessness, and overweening pride in his exalted position. Badly served he may well have been, and all through his life it was among his chiefest misfortunes that the execution of his plans had to be confided to agents quite unworthy to give proper effect to them. But with all his love of joustings and hunting, events show that he seldom neglected his serious business.

Men lived short lives in the Middle Ages, and correspondingly began their active career at an exceedingly early age. The mediaeval prince or noble was often a warrior, a practised statesman, a husband and a father when still little more than a mere boy. This was the case with Edward. He was only eight when his father began to think of providing him with a wife. But the negotiations entered upon in 1247 for a marriage between the young Edward and a daughter of the Duke of Brabant led to no result. When Edward was about thirteen, fresh marriage negotiations were begun with Alfonso X., King of Castile. This prince was a descendant of Eleanor, daughter of Henry II., from whose marriage with King Alfonso VIII. of Castile had resulted a long and intimate connection between England and Castile, which coloured the whole of our foreign policy up to the Reformation. But marriage connections involved not only relations of kinship but unpleasant claims of right. Alfonso X. was the most powerful of the Spanish kings, an able, vigorous, active, and aggressive ruler. The compilation of the code of the

Siete Partidas made his reign an epoch in the history of Castile, while his adventurous disposition led him later to accept the doubtful advantage of election to the Holy Roman Empire in rivalry to Edward's uncle, Earl Richard of Cornwall. The same restless and aggressive spirit Alfonso now showed by entertaining the appeals of the rebellious Gascon subjects of the English King, who called upon him to vindicate his claims to the duchy as the heir of Eleanor of Guienne. It was even believed in England that Alfonso proposed to invade England with an army of Castilians and Saracens. Henry thought it wise to remove the possibilities of a conflict, and restore the old friendly relations with Castile by a proposal to marry Edward to Alfonso's half-sister Eleanor, the daughter of King Ferdinand the Saint by his second wife Joan of Ponthieu, a young girl already reputed to possess great beauty, goodness, and sound sense, and who was, moreover, in right of her mother, heiress of the rich counties of Ponthieu and Montreuil in Western Picardy. That Edward himself might not go landless to the marriage, Henry conferred upon his son such extensive territories that he became, men said, no better than a mutilated king. In 1253 Henry sailed to Gascony, hoping to appease some disturbances that were then raging there, and conclude the match. Edward, who was taken to Portsmouth to see his father depart, stood weeping upon the shore as the ship sailed away, and would not leave it as long as a sail could still be seen. Queen Eleanor remained in England to look after her son and the realm. The next year the marriage treaty was signed, and in the early summer of 1254 Edward sailed with his mother and his uncle,

Archbishop Boniface of Canterbury, to join his father in Gascony. In August he went to Alfonso's court at Burgos to carry on his suit in person. His mother still accompanied him. Alfonso received them with great pomp and festivity, examined the youth in his skill and knowledge, and conferred upon him the honour of knighthood. In October he was married to Eleanor at the monastery of Las Huelgas, and shortly afterwards returned with his wife to Bordeaux, whence a year later they returned to England. The marriage thus concluded between the royal children proved one of the happiest in English history. Edward and Eleanor rivalled Henry and Eleanor in the warmth of their attachment and the purity of their domestic lives. They were scarcely ever separated, Eleanor making it her pride to share in the toils and dangers of her husband. On her death, after thirty-five years of happy wedlock, Edward experienced the most poignant grief. His whole character changed for the worse after the removal of the faithful partner of his youth and early manhood.

In the thirteenth century a king's son did not form a member of a special royal caste. He had no distinctive title and was brought up very much like any other young man of high birth. The old English word "Ætheling" had ceased to be used as the appropriate designation of the son of a crowned and anointed king. The vaguer modern word "prince" did not come into use for many centuries later. The eldest son of the English king had no higher title than the vague appellation of "lord," which he shared with a whole host of feudal chieftains, great and small, with the bishops, abbots, judges, and even the masters and doctors of the universities. To speak of our hero as "Prince Edward" is an anachronism, though sometimes it is a convenient one. Contemporaries were content to call him "the Lord Edward, the first-born son of the King," or, more shortly, "the Lord Edward." It is best to imitate their example.

The provision for a mediaeval king's son was not made by grants and pensions from a civil list, but by the conference of large estates and territories, which he was expected to manage as a landlord, if not also to rule as a feudal chieftain. It was only through the successful administration of his domains that he could expect to get an adequate income for himself. The privilege of receiving the revenue of his appanage thus involved the duty of hard work in its government. It was, moreover, a very common practice all over Europe to confer upon the youthful heir some outlying and semi-independent portion of the royal dominions that was not strictly a part of the main kingdom, and which gave the young prince a wide and free field to learn how to govern and prepare himself for the larger task of ruling the kingdom itself. A familiar though later example is the grant to the French king's heirs of the outlying district of Dauphiny, whence their well-known title of Dauphin. In the next century it became the custom in England to confer on the king's eldest son the Principality of Wales. But long before this had grown into a regular fashion, long before the Principality was in the king's hands to bestow, a similar practice had arisen. The lavish grants of territory made, as we have seen, to Edward between 1252 and 1254 had not simply the object of providing him with an adequate revenue to keep his court in due state with his young wife. They were also made with the design of giving him experience as a ruler in those districts of his father's dominions where the most valuable experience could be got. The ample provision made for Edward included indeed certain English cities such as Bristol, Stamford, and Grantham. But these were but an insignificant portion of the whole. The real importance of the grants lies in the gift to Edward of all Ireland, the earldom of Chester, the king's lands in Wales, the islands of Jersey and Guernsey with their dependencies, and the whole of Gascony with the island of Oléron, and whatever rights the king still had over all the other lands taken from his predecessors by the kings of France. It was, in short, the transference from Henry to Edward of all those parts of the British Islands outside England itself where the English King had any claim to rule. Along with these outlying dependencies, went every vestige that remained of the Norman inheritance of William the Bastard and the Aquitanian inheritance of Eleanor of Guienne. Edward was thus made the representative of the claims still brought forward from time to time for the restitution of the great Angevin Empire, reduced to insignificance by the heedless folly of John and the watchful aggressions of the French kings. The results of both series of grants were of unspeakable importance for the future history of Edward, and indeed for the future destinies of the British Islands. It was perhaps the greatest work of Edward's life to revive and extend the policy of the great West Saxon kings before the Conquest of reducing the whole British Islands under the rule of the English King. The firmness and clearness with which Edward persisted in this policy may in no small measure be attributed to his early experience as ruler of Wales, Chester, and Ireland. Hardly second in importance to the imperial schemes of Edward in Britain was the firm policy with which he upheld England in a foremost place in the councils of Europe. This again can be traced back to his early experiences as a ruler of the English King's dominions in France. That he thought the real acquisition of Wales, Scotland, and Ireland more important and more worthy objects than vain attempts to renew the Angevin Empire on the Continent is perhaps almost equally true of his later policy. His early Gascon training gave him opportunities for reforming the institutions and developing the resources of his great feudal duchy, while it could not but convince him of the real limitations imposed upon his power in the south of France.

It is important to realise the exact position of the lands made over by Henry to Edward when the young prince was started on his active career. The appanage he received was a large one, but it was so unprofitable that Henry had to promise his son that the value of the lands settled on him should not fall short of 15,000 marks. In fact, Edward's whole lordship was in such a disturbed state that the maintenance of law and order within it could only be assured by means of lavish subsidies from the royal Exchequer. Such subsidies Henry was in no condition to make. The impossible task was therefore assigned to Edward and his advisers of reducing Ireland, Wales, and Gascony with their own resources; while at the same time it was necessary that

14

sufficient revenue should be derived from these poor and disturbed regions to provide for the support of their lord's household.

Ireland was of all Edward's dominions in the most hopeless position. The first energies of the Norman conquerors of the twelfth century had been exhausted, and, though the great Norman houses still ruled extensive territories, they had begun to experience the attraction of Irish influence, and besides the hibernicisation of the Norman lords, the native septs were coming down from the hills and disputing with their new masters the domination of the plain country. But the power of the English crown had become insignificant alike over Norman lord and Irish chieftain. Edward's deputy at Dublin could command the obedience of neither. The Celtic chieftains upheld the tribal anarchy of the old Irish septs. The Norman lords saw their ideal of government in a political feudalism which gave the great landlord every regalian right, and necessarily involved the complete disintegration of all central authority. The central power was weak, foreign, and unpopular. These complicated evils had reduced the unhappy island to a state of confusion almost worse than that which had prevailed in the wild times of independence, before Strongbow and his associates had crossed the St. George's Channel. To grapple seriously with such difficulties was beyond the strength of Edward's advisers. They paid little attention to Ireland, preferring to concentrate their efforts on the smaller and more accessible territory of Wales.

The plans of Edward's advisers in Wales for the reduction of Wales were made possible by the grant of the great earldom of Chester. Ever since the Conquest Chester had been a district standing by itself. It was a palatine earldom, set up by the Conqueror to keep in check the wild Welshmen. With this object the Earl was given an almost absolute control of the civil and military resources of his shire. His duties to the Crown were discharged by simple homage and service. He held Cheshire as freely by his sword as the King held England by his crown. This position is in all respects analogous to that of the practically independent feudal chieftains of France or Germany. The result was that Cheshire became a great military state. Its population were famed for their violence, turbulence, and martial powers. Headed by their fierce lords, the Cheshiremen had conquered nearly all Wales between the Dee and the Conway, though a later wave of Welsh enthusiasm had driven the invaders back almost to the walls of Chester. But the great line of Earls of Chester was now extinct. The bestowal of lapsed fiefs was among the most important of the prerogatives of the Crown. It was no small gain to the royal cause that Henry was thus able to invest his son with the rich, fair, and fertile Palatinate. It involved revenue, soldiers, influence, dignity, and the status of the greatest of English earls. It gave the new Earl of Chester means to make good the vaguer grant of "Wales."

Wales included all the exceptional jurisdictions of the western peninsula, largely but by no means exclusively inhabited by Welshmen. In thinking of the Wales of the thirteenth century, we must forget the modern boundary which separates the twelve or thirteen counties of the Wales of to-day from the modern England. This boundary goes no farther back than the reign of Henry VIII. Thirteenth-century Wales included much that is now England, while some parts of what is now Wales were then English ground. Beyond the vague and undefined western limits of Cheshire, Shropshire, Herefordshire, and Gloucestershire, everything was Wales.

Before the Norman Conquest Wales had been ruled by a swarm of petty Celtic chieftains, whose energies were consumed in fruitless fights with each other, the true "battles of kites and crows" of British history. All owed a nominal allegiance to the English kings, but this lax feudal tie did not prevent them plundering and devastating the English border whenever a fair opportunity was offered. But the strong rule of William I. and his sons brought about a great change. The Norman Conquest of England was followed by the Norman Conquest of Wales. A swarm of Norman adventurers crossed over the border and drove the Welsh from the fair plains to the barren uplands. The mutual jealousies of the petty Welsh kings and princes made national union impossible, and without union effectual resistance to the Normans was hardly to be thought of. But the Norman Conquerors were as little united as the Welsh that they displaced. As in Ireland, the ideal of feudal lord and clan chieftain had this in common that it involved an infinite division of political power. The Norman conquerors of Wales fought for their own hands and were almost independent of the kings of England. They set up therefore a whole host of petty states, over which they ruled like little kings. These small Norman principalities on Welsh ground were known as the Lordships Marcher, and the whole district as the Marches of Wales,

17

though the original idea of the March as a border was largely lost sight of in an age when the Welsh Marches included the districts so remote from the English border as a great part of the modern Pembrokeshire. The most important of the Lordships Marcher of Wales were the palatine earldom of Pembroke and the great lordship of Glamorgan, whose lords were not called Earls only because they had already that title from their English earldom of Gloucester. Next in importance was the lordship of Brecon, an appendage to the earldom of Hereford. More to the north the great family of Mortimer bore sway in Shropshire and the Middle Marches. The Four Cantreds of Perveddwlad (the plain country) Rhos, Rhuvoniog, Duffryn Clwyd, and Tygeingl, which roughly corresponded to the modern Denbighshire and Flintshire, depended on the Earls of Chester. All southern and eastern Wales was thus March ground.

The Norman Conquest also indirectly affected Welsh Wales. It finally forced the native Welsh to unite among each other as the only alternative to complete subjection. A great national and literary revival broke out in Celtic Wales. The lords of Gwynedd, whose rule included the mountain fastnesses of Snowdon and Merioneth and the rich corn-lands of Anglesey, became the leaders of the Welsh national revival. Bit by bit the old jealousies of tribe and tribe, of north and south, were removed. At last all Welshmen looked up to the lords of Snowdon as the champions of the national cause against the restless and oppressive French invaders. Llywelyn ab Iorwerth, the greatest of Welsh princes, cleverly used this new feeling of national unity to extend his north

Welsh principality at the expense of the now divided and quarrelsome Marchers. He pushed his successes eastwards to the walls of Chester, and southwards to the shores of Carmarthen Bay, thus forcing a wedge of Welsh territory through parts of the modern Cardiganshire and Carmarthenshire, though the royal stronghold of Carmarthen still checked his onward progress. But while his praises were chanted by the native bards as the hero of the Cymric race, Llywelyn never forgot that he was not only a national Welsh prince but a great feudal English lord. He accordingly allied himself with the baronial opposition to English kings, and took a prominent part in the struggle for Magna Charta, clauses of which ensured him many important privileges. Before his death in 1240 he was proud to call himself prince of all Wales. His son David (1240-1246), born of his English wife Joan, King John's bastard daughter, was hardly strong enough to uphold Llywelyn's power. But after his death a full-blooded Welshman again acquired the Principality. The new prince was David's nephew Llywelyn ab Gruffydd, the son of Llywelyn ab Iorwerth's favourite son by a Welsh mother. For nearly forty years (1246-1282) Llywelyn ab Gruffydd strove to maintain the policy, both national and feudal, of his grandfather. But at the time we are now dealing with he had not attained any very great measure of success.

The twofold division of Wales into the Principality and the Marches must never be lost sight of if we wish to understand the Welsh policy of Edward I. We must remember that the Principality did not then mean, as it does in its loose modern use, the whole of Wales, but strictly the districts ruled over by the Prince of Wales, Llywelyn ab Gruffydd. At this time that region roughly comprised what now constitutes the three shires of Anglesea, Carnarvon, and Merioneth. The Four Cantreds and the lands between the Dovey and Carmarthen Bay had fallen into the hands of the English king, and were now the main districts granted to Edward. Edward's Welsh lands therefore included a great deal of what is now Denbighshire and Flintshire, and of what is now Cardiganshire and Carmarthenshire. But beyond these royal dominions were the Marches, the term meaning not simply the border districts but all those parts of Wales ruled over by Norman lords on feudal principles. A few of these may have fallen by lapse into Edward's hands, but the real significance of Henry's grant was that it included all the recent acquisitions from the restless Princes of Wales.

Edward had already vigorous and able, though fierce and unscrupulous, advisers. His ministers now formed a scheme of introducing English institutions into their master's lands in Wales. The current phrase (well known in Ireland down to the seventeenth century) for bringing English law into a country was to make the district in question "shire ground." Edward's advisers therefore sought to attach the Four Cantreds to the county of Chester, while they set up a new shire of which the centre was Carmarthen, but which was for convenience sake split up later into the counties of Cardigan and Carmarthen. So sovereign a remedy was English law considered for the chronic anarchy of Wales, that some Welshmen had actually begged Henry to introduce it into their land. But the whole weight of national feeling clung to the rough rude laws of Howel the Good, which the Welsh regarded as the basis of their jurisprudence. While Edward's officers were establishing their hundredmoots and their shiremoots, his Welsh subjects took counsel together and declared that they would never give up the laws of their fathers. The violence and greed with which Edward's deputy, Geoffrey Langley, sought to bring in the new system completed their disgust. In their despair they turned to Llywelyn, who gleefully welcomed a chance of winning back the dominions of his grandfather. In the autumn of 1256 Llywelyn's troops poured down from the heights of Snowdon over the Four Cantreds. The plain country submitted through the goodwill of the native inhabitants for the invaders. Two castles alone, Dyserth (near Rhyl) and Deganwy (near Llandudno), held out for Earl Edward.

Edward hurried from the delights of the tourney and tiltyard to defend his inheritance. But he had no money and no men to cope with the trained warriors of Llywelyn. He soon exhausted a loan that he obtained from his rich uncle Richard, and earnestly besought his father to come to his assistance. "What business is it of mine?" answered Henry; "I have given you the land. You must act for yourself." But next year Henry was prevailed upon to accompany Edward in an expedition to North Wales. Father and son penetrated to the sorely beleaguered castle of Deganwy, where they spent some time. But on their retirement the Welsh again became masters of all the land but a few castles. It was Edward's first campaign, an inglorious beginning for so great a martial career. But it gave the young earl valuable experience in Welsh

21

warfare, and may well have first opened his eyes to the weakness and incompetence of his father as a king. It left him discredited, overwhelmed with debt, and eager to barter away part of his patrimony for ready money. But it showed him the way by which Llywelyn might some day be conquered, and it showed him still more clearly how Wales, if conquered, ought to be ruled. The germ of all Edward's later Welsh policy lies in his early attempt to establish the shire system in his Welsh estates.

Gascony, Guienne, or Aquitaine (the terms at this period at least are practically synonymous) was no less than Wales the object of Edward's special concern. It included all that remained in English hands of the vast possessions which Eleanor of Poitou had brought to her husband Henry II. It was a land of great wealth and prosperity, a land of vineyards and rich corn-fields, watered by noble rivers, with many a wealthy and flourishing town, and a great band of warlike, turbulent, lawless nobility, in whom the wild, fierce spirit still lived that had in an earlier age found an undying expression in the songs of Bertrand de Born, and among whom Richard the Lion Heart had found the ideals of his restless, adventurous, purposeless life. Cut off from France by language, manners, sympathies, and traditions, the Gascons were content with the rule of their English dukes, because they were so far off that they had little reason to fear them, and because they found in England the best and readiest market for their wines. But the towns were little republics, almost as free and as self-contained as the great cities of Italy, and like them torn by fierce factions, such as the Rosteins and Colons of Bordeaux, and the popular and aristocratic parties of Bayonne. The feudal nobles, in their hill castles on the slopes of the Pyrenees and Cevennes, were for all practical purposes independent. Chief among them was Gaston, Viscount of Beam, the uncle of Queen Eleanor, and the greediest, cruellest, most desperate, and turbulent of men. Strong neighbours watched eagerly the chronic tumults within the duchy, hoping to derive therefrom some advantage to themselves. Of these the most dangerous were the King of Navarre, and Alfonso, Count of Poitiers and Toulouse, the brother of Louis IX. of France, actual possessor of the northern and eastern portions of Henry II.'s Aquitanian inheritance, and the pioneer of North French influence in the Languedoc. Against such complicated troubles, weak King Henry had been able to make no way at all, until in 1248 he had made Simon of Montfort seneschal or governor of Gascony. Earl Simon's strong, fierce, vigorous rule soon began to work a great change; but he was reckless of his means and strove to do everything at once. He had poor support from England, and soon raised up a whole host of enemies in Gascony, who overwhelmed the English king with complaints and eagerly demanded the recall of the Earl of Leicester.

This was the state of things when Edward first received the grant of Gascony from his father. His uncle and godfather still remained seneschal, acting henceforth for the son and not for the father. At first the king encouraged Simon, hoping that he would prepare the way for Edward's future rule. "You shall receive," he wrote to his brother-in-law, "from us and our heir a recompense worthy of your services." It was left to the Gascon towns first to bring Edward into that opposition to Earl Simon which was to colour the whole of his future life. They hated Leicester, and strove to set up their new lord against his fierce deputy. "We beg your Majesty," wrote the deputies of the flourishing city of Bazas, "to drive Earl Simon from Gascony, and send us your son Edward, our lord, who will find us all in peace." Henry in response confirmed his grant to Edward, but with his usual weakness again sent back Simon as governor, though plainly showing that he had no longer his full confidence. When Henry was in Gascony in 1253 Simon was still his seneschal; but next year he was dismissed in disgrace, and, filled with a burning sense of wrong and hatred, plunged eagerly into the camp of the baronial opposition in England. In 1254 and 1255 Edward himself lived mostly in Gascony. Here too he acquired valuable experience. Apart from the importance of his Gascon rule in first bringing out his opposition to Leicester, it taught him lessons as to how the English king's lands in France should be governed, which in later years bore him excellent fruit. It, moreover, gave him that insight into south French and Spanish politics which qualified him to fulfil the leading part in those regions to which in after years he was called. On his return to England he did not forget the interests of his Gascon subjects. In 1261 he drew up an elaborate series of statutes for Bordeaux which, while taking away from the citizens the right of choosing their own mayor, gave them in compensation full protection from the exactions of the royal officials. The need of such protection had been brought home to Edward by the bitter complaints which the wine merchants of Bordeaux now presented to him of the ruin to their trade caused by the exactions of the king's officials. Edward eagerly espoused their cause, and plainly told his father that such exactions must cease. For the first time his sense of the impolicy of Henry's conduct prompted him to break through the strong ties of affection which bound him to the fondest and most indulgent of fathers. Henry was bitterly offended. "My own flesh and blood," he exclaimed with a sigh, "are assailing me; the times of my grandfather, whose children waged war against him, are surely coming back." Nothing shows more clearly the impracticable and hopeless attitude of the old king than these foolish and petulant remarks. But the time was coming when Edward's faithfulness to his father was to endure far sterner trials than this. The time of his apprenticeship was over. With the beginning of the great dispute between Henry and his barons, Edward enters into his real political career.

CHAPTER II

EDWARD AND THE BARONS' WARS
1258-1267

THE personal government of Henry III. had now lasted for more than five and twenty years. Year after year his weak and nerveless rule had become worse. He gave the nation neither strong government nor popular control. A feeble attempt at despotism had brought about a chronic state of anarchy. Extravagance, nepotism, incompetence had reigned supreme. Many and loud had been the protests that the wiser among the churchmen and the nobler among the baronage had raised against the weak king's misdoings. But the tyranny of Henry was not of that severe and grinding kind which invites immediate and strenuous resistance even at the expense of revolution. And the opposition was wanting in unity of policy and in leaders of capacity. Thus it was that, despite the protests of the gallant Richard Marshal, the despairing lamentations of the sainted Edmund of Abingdon, the more manly denunciations of Bishop Grosseteste, and the spirited action of Earl Richard of Cornwall, Henry was still able to go on in his evil ways. But new complications now presented themselves which at last brought about the final crisis. The return of Simon de Montfort from Gascony, thoroughly and for ever at feud with his royal brother-in-law, gave the opposition a leader of matchless ability, resourcefulness, energy, and

26

daring. The vain attempt of Henry to procure for his second son Edmund the crown of Sicily had imposed a new and a crushing burden upon the scanty resources of the kingdom. The popes, who used Edmund as a tool to drive out the heirs of their hated enemy, Frederick of Hohenstaufen, from the Sicilian throne, pledged Henry's credit to the uttermost, and sent legates to England to demand the fulfilment of his promises. This led to the famous Parliaments of Barons of 1258. At London, in the spring, Henry was forced to accept a commission of reform. At Oxford, in the summer, a new constitution was drawn up and forced upon the reluctant monarch. By the Provisions of Oxford the whole power of the Crown was put into the hands of a committee of fifteen barons. The king's household was set in order, his alien kinsmen and favourites were driven beyond sea, and the custody of royal castles entrusted to Englishmen alone. A sweeping scheme of further reformation was drawn up for the future. A few months' vigorous action reduced the would-be despot to a position of utter powerlessness.

Edward was now in his twentieth year. It is probable that he was already dimly conscious of his father's deficiencies, but his filial affection and his pride of power alike prompted him to vigorously oppose the audacious designs of the barons. But he soon found himself swept away by the torrent. In vain he set himself against the expulsion of his familiar friends and companions, his uncles the Lusignans. The barons forced him to take part in the siege of Winchester Castle, from which his Poitevin uncles made their last unavailing resistance. After their expulsion he gave his reluctant oath to observe the Provisions of

Oxford. It must have been a bitter humiliation to him to be compelled to accept the appointment of four baronial councillors, specially commissioned to reform his turbulent and disorderly household. But with all his loyalty he could not sacrifice enough to satisfy the exacting affection of his foolish father. A hot quarrel broke out between the king and his son, though it was soon ended by an affectionate reconciliation in the chapter-house at Winchester. Yet each outburst of foolish petulance on Henry's part could not but be a fresh inducement to Edward to take up a line of his own. In his passive action in 1258 he had abundant opportunity to win fresh experience. The removal of his Poitevin and Provençal kinsfolk threw him back on more English and more capable advisers. Next year he began to play an independent part.

The Provisions of Oxford had not satisfied everybody. The revolution had been carried out by a ring of great earls and barons, who thought, like the Whigs of the eighteenth century, that the transference of power to themselves had made the constitution so perfect that further improvements were not to be hoped for. This was not the view of the Earl of Leicester, but as a new man and a foreigner his influence was far inferior to that of Richard of Clare, the Earl of Gloucester, whose vast possessions and vigorous personal character made him the natural head of the English aristocracy. But new classes of the community now entered for the first time into the arena of practical politics. The country gentlemen of knightly rank, the natural leaders of the unrepresented masses of the nation, had already begun to get political experience from the new fashion of summoning knights of the shire to treat with the king in general parliaments. They now began to murmur loudly that the old grievances under which the nation had groaned so long were in no wise removed by the change of leaders. These men, "the community of the bachelorhood of England," addressed to Edward a long petition for further reform, and denounced the barons for breaking their word and working merely "for their own good and the harm of the king." Edward answered that he was ready to die for the good of the commonwealth, but that though he had sworn to the Provisions with the utmost unwillingness, he was resolved to keep his oath. He took up their cause with his usual impetuous ardour, and thus dissociated himself from the mere courtier party. One result of his energetic action was a further though small instalment of reform in the Provisions of Westminster. It is significant that while Henry simply swore to observe these Provisions, Edward added to his acceptance an oath that he would advise and aid Earl Simon against all men. Perhaps the most important immediate result of this movement was that it brought Edward into temporary relations with his uncle Montfort. It is hard to say that Edward's object was simply to divide his father's enemies and so break down the slavery to which the Crown had been subjected, though no doubt this result did follow from his action. But for a time there was a complete breach between Edward and Henry, a complete harmony of action between the king's son and Earl Simon. Queen Eleanor, who could not forgive her son's desertion of her Provençal kinsfolk, stirred up Henry against Edward. Gloucester, now Simon's declared enemy, did his best to widen the breach. Something like civil war seemed likely to break out between the followers of Gloucester and those of Edward. For five weeks and more the Londoners sought to keep the peace by closing their gates and guarding them with an armed force.

The absence of Henry in France, whither he had gone to negotiate a peace with his brother-in-law St. Louis, still further complicated matters. There Henry signed a treaty by which he formally renounced all claims on Normandy and Poitou, thus giving up those pretensions which a few years before he had so solemnly handed over to his son. Simon hotly opposed the peace. It is not likely that Edward was very favourable to it. But both Edward and Simon became parties to the treaty, and solemnly renounced their share in the abandoned claims.

In the spring of 1260 things got worse. Henry and Eleanor were informed, as they were travelling back to England, that Edward had formed a conspiracy with the barons to depose his father, and that the king on his arrival home would be forthwith hurried into captivity. The story was an outrageous fiction, but it thoroughly frightened Henry, who lingered on the French shore of the Channel, fearing to cross the straits. At last the timely intervention of Richard of Cornwall, now King of the Romans, convinced Henry that his suspicions were exaggerated. Henry was much offended with Edward. On his arrival in London he sternly refused to see his son, who was lodging with Simon outside the city walls. But the weak head and good heart of the king could not long endure such unnatural estrangement. "Do not let my son appear before me," he exclaimed, "for if I see him, I shall not be able to refrain from kissing him." After a fortnight father and son were reconciled. Edward gradually dropped his connections with Simon, though he kept up his feud with Gloucester until the death of Earl Richard in 1262. Disgusted at the troubles that had resulted from his first active intervention in politics, Edward withdrew for a time from public affairs, and again sought distraction in his favourite amusement of the tiltyard. He now went to France for a great tournament, in which he came off badly. Again in 1262 he went abroad for the same purpose. He proved victor in several mock encounters, but in one he received a serious wound.

Henry III. had long wearied of his inglorious degradation at the hands of the Fifteen, and had for some time been engaged in secret intrigues against the constitution which he had sworn to observe. His last scruples were removed when two successive popes absolved both him and his son Edward from their oaths. On 2nd May 1262 Henry solemnly proclaimed to the sheriffs the tidings of his absolution from his obligations. But later in the year, on learning that the young Earl Gilbert, who had just succeeded his father in the Gloucester estates and title, had thrown himself warmly on the side of Leicester, Henry again confirmed the Provisions. A few months later he was again at work undermining the new constitution. By Whitsuntide 1263 open civil war had broken out.

Edward spent the early part of 1263 in Paris. But the tidings came that Llywelyn of Wales had again invaded his Welsh estates, and after hurriedly collecting a body of foreign mercenaries, he hastened back to England, and was engaged until Whitsuntide in a fruitless campaign against the Welsh. Meanwhile the civil war had broken out, hastened by the refusal of the young Earl of Gloucester to take the oath of allegiance to Edward, which Henry, with singular want of tact, now insisted upon imposing upon the magnates. Edward threw himself into Windsor Castle, while Simon raised an army and encamped at Isleworth, a village on the Middlesex bank of the Thames, just below Richmond, hoping thus to separate Edward at Windsor from Henry and Eleanor, who had taken refuge in the Tower of London from the fury of the Londoners, who were nearly all staunch partisans of Earl Simon. One day Eleanor, apparently with the object of joining Edward at Windsor, took boat and attempted to pass underneath London bridge on her upward journey. But a great mob of the London rabble thronged the bridge, reviled her as a traitress, and an adulterous foreigner, and pelted her barge with stones, mud, rotten eggs, and all manner of filth. She was soon forced back to the Tower. The incident is mainly memorable for its effect on Edward, who bitterly resented the foul indignities heaped upon Eleanor, and became a sworn foe to London and its liberties for the rest of his life. Edward now applied himself with extraordinary dexterity to win over Leicester's followers, and succeeded in creating a strong party for himself, of which the backbone was the fierce Lords Marcher of Wales, who might well have looked upon Edward as their natural leader, and who had already fought by his side against Llywelyn. In revenge Simon forced a close alliance with the Prince of Wales, and promised him his daughter as a wife. Thus Llywelyn fought for the baronial cause, just as his grandfather Llywelyn ab Iorwerth had joined the nobles arrayed against John in the first struggle for the Charter. Meanwhile fresh truces were made, only to be broken; and fresh parliaments assembled, only to be dissolved amidst riot and confusion. Edward's tactics had so far succeeded that neither side was strong enough to get the better of the other. At last, in December, all parties agreed to submit their disputes to the arbitration of St. Louis.

Edward sailed with his father for France, suffering severely during his passage from the storms of December. Early in 1264 the French king, as might have been expected, annulled the Provisions, and declared on all points in favour of Henry III. Leicester, as might equally have been anticipated, refused to be bound by the arbitration to which he had sworn. On his taking up arms, Edward hurried back to England to defend his father's cause. He was already the practical leader of the royalists, and the outbreak of civil war now forced him still more fully to the front. He alone could take the lead in the king's council, for he alone could form a royalist party. There had been no party for Henry as long as he ruled through foreigners and favourites, any more than there was any party for Charles I. in the days of Ship Money, the Bishops' Wars, and the first session of the Long Parliament. Edward did effectually for his father what Hyde and Falkland did less successfully for Charles I. He showed the nation that Earl Simon was not the only reformer, and that the mass of the barons were not reformers at all. He upheld a constitutional royalism which allowed for national progress but discouraged revolution. But the bad traditions of long years of misgovernment still clave to his following, and the hot revengeful fire of

33

youth still coloured the political conduct of Edward with personal motives. Despite his gallant fight he did not this time succeed, and it was well for England that the early failure of Edward preceded his later triumph.

The campaign of 1264 was begun by Earl Simon, who, half despairing at the threatened break up of his party through Edward's intrigues, was resolved to conquer or perish. "Though all men quit me," he exclaimed, "I will remain with my four sons and fight for the good cause which I have sworn to defend for the honour of Holy Church and the welfare of the realm." While Simon himself marshalled the levies of the south, his eldest son Henry operated in the west in conjunction with Llywelyn of Wales, and his second son Simon raised a force in the Midlands at Kenilworth.

Edward hurried to the west, to join his friends the Lords Marcher in the fight against Henry Montfort and Llywelyn. He strove to throw himself into Gloucester Castle, the town, which commanded the passage over the Severn, being already in the hands of the barons. But though he gained his point, his numbers were too small to enable him to maintain his position, and he was forced to beg for a truce from his cousin. Henry Montfort chivalrously, or rashly, granted an armistice. But on the withdrawal of Henry to Kenilworth Edward treacherously broke the truce, and regained possession of the town. Master of the chief crossing over the Lower Severn, he could now turn his attention to the more general campaign. He soon joined his father at Oxford, where he drove out all the masters and scholars, who, headed by their

Chancellor, Thomas of Cantilupe, were enthusiastic partisans of the popular cause. Thence father and son marched against Northampton, where the younger Simon now was. Edward easily captured the town and took his cousin prisoner, having great trouble to save his life in the wild confusion of the storm. He now devastated the earldom of Leicester with fire and sword. But the royal forces were soon called off to the south, where Rochester, the key of Kent, was in danger of falling into the hands of Earl Simon.

The king easily relieved Rochester, and wandered aimlessly through Kent and Sussex, seeking, though with little success, to win over the hostile Cinque Ports, and striving to open communications with Queen Eleanor, who was collecting an army of foreign mercenaries in the Flemish harbours. But his soldiers suffered severely from lack of food and forage. As his troops plodded wearily through the deep lanes and dense copses of the Weald, they were much harassed by Simon's light armed Welsh archers, who lurked in every hedge and thicket and inflicted severe losses upon them. At last the weary host rested at Lewes. Edward took up his quarters in the castle to the north of the town, while his father, with whom was his uncle Richard, King of the Romans, occupied the priory, on the southern side of Lewes.

Earl Simon had retired from Rochester to the capital, whence he marched south with an army reinforced by a host of Londoners, all fresh and eager for battle, though but little accustomed to warfare. On 13th May he slept at Fletching, a village nine miles to the north of Lewes.

Thence, early on the morning of 14th May, Montfort marched across the South Downs, hoping to surprise the town.

Lewes is situated on the right bank of the Ouse, which here makes a bend that almost encircles the town. To the west and north the South Downs sink gradually down in the form of a natural amphitheatre until they form the gap in which the town is built. The army of the barons swept swiftly across the bare rolling chalk downs, hoping to attack the castle and priory simultaneously. But their movements were discovered, and the royalists poured out of the town, ready to fight out the battle upon the open plain. Simon fixed his standard upon the hill, hoping that its conspicuous position would tempt the royalist attack. But while he gathered the mass of his army on the right wing which operated from the west against the defenders of the priory, he massed around the standard the untrained though enthusiastic Londoners. All turned out as Simon had expected. Edward, the real general of the royalists, at once fell into the trap, and charged with the flower of the host the dense masses grouped around the Earl's standard. With him was his gallant cousin Henry of Almaine. The Londoners were smitten with panic and fled in confusion; while Edward, delighted to revenge on the citizens the insults they had heaped upon his mother, pursued them vigorously for four miles, giving no quarter and inflicting terrible losses upon them. At last, tired out with slaughter, his weary troops marched back into Lewes. But they found that in their absence Earl Simon had forced the royal positions, captured the priory in which the king had taken up his quarters, and driven the King of the Romans to take refuge in a mill,

36

where he was soon forced to surrender. Edward's troops now dispersed in a panic. Next day the Mise of Lewes was drawn up, by which the Provisions of Oxford were renewed, and Henry again forced to delegate his power to a baronial committee. One of the articles provided that Edward and Henry of Almaine were to be given up as hostages for the good behaviour of the Lords Marcher, who were still in arms in the west. On 16th May Edward surrendered. He and his cousin were put under the care of Henry Montfort, who shut them up at Dover and treated them as captives rather than hostages, and less honourably than was becoming. Edward was afterwards removed to Kenilworth, where his aunt, the Countess of Leicester, seems to have dealt with him more considerately than her son.

A new constitution was soon drawn up which put all power in the hands of three grand electors, and their nominees a council of nine. But the Marchers still held out; Queen Eleanor and her mercenaries still threatened invasion, and the pope fulminated anathemas against Simon and his adherents. Accordingly Simon found it necessary to repose further trust in the people. Hence he summoned his famous Parliament of January 1265, in which for the first time knights of the shire and representatives of the burgesses sat side by side, and deliberated in common with the bishops and barons who favoured the popular party. No one now thinks that Simon's parliamentary convention was the first House of Commons, but it marks an important era in the development of our parliamentary institutions. Besides being the completest Parliament that had hitherto been summoned, it is the first popular Parliament consciously gathered together to deal with a great political crisis. It is not too much, therefore, to regard it as the first occasion on which the rulers of England deliberately took the people into partnership with them. It taught a lesson that was never effaced from the mind of the impatient prisoner at Kenilworth.

In this Parliament it was arranged that Edward was to surrender his earldom of Chester to Leicester and to be speedily released from captivity. But the dark ambitions of Leicester and the brutal violence of his sons had again split up the popular party. No one could ever work long with Earl Simon. Gilbert of Gloucester's youthful enthusiasm for his brilliant mentor had now worn off. After a violent quarrel he retired in anger to his estates and joined the Marchers. Leicester accordingly marched to the west, taking Edward with him by way of precaution. About Whitsuntide Edward was at Hereford, under the custody of Thomas of Clare, the brother of the Earl of Gloucester, by whose mediation a secret understanding was arrived at for his escape. One day Edward went outside the city, attended by Thomas and a few knights, for the sake of taking exercise. The conversation turned on horsemanship, and Edward, as if to try their paces, rode in turn all the horses of the party. At last he found out which steed was the swiftest and strongest, and, mounting hastily upon it, rode off as hard as he could. His guardians soon saw that they were duped, and galloped after him in pursuit. But Edward had got too good a start and was too well mounted to run much risk of capture. Before long he joined a band of armed Marchers, who were waiting for him in a wood, and conducted him safely to the Mortimers' stronghold of Wigmore. He now made terms with the Earl of Gloucester. At Ludlow Edward solemnly swore that, if he obtained the victory, he would cause to be observed all the good old laws of the land, would do away with all evil customs, expel all aliens from the king's castles, court, and council, and take care that England should be ruled by Englishmen. It was an eventful moment. This treaty of Ludlow, marking the formal acceptance by Edward of the popular programme, completed the transformation of parties which, through Edward's influence, had been slowly working ever since 1259. Henceforth it was not Leicester but Edward who best represents the cause of orderly national progress. Leicester with all his greatness had made himself impossible, and his designs were more and more suspected. Henry becomes henceforth a mere puppet in his son's hands. And Edward, in taking his promises, had no mere intention of outbidding the rival faction or "dishing the Whigs." His whole future shows that he had convinced himself that the policy he swore to uphold at Ludlow was the right one. Henceforth the English monarchy becomes both national and progressive.

Leicester soon saw that the game was up, but manfully resolved to die fighting for the good old cause. A vast army gathered together under the standards of Edward and Gloucester. By the capture of Gloucester town, they hemmed up Leicester on the right bank of the Severn, and cut him off from his son Simon, who was collecting another army in the Midlands. While Leicester was marching wearily up and down the Severn, hoping to find a passage, Edward on 1st August surprised the younger Simon at Kenilworth, and almost annihilated his army, though he failed to capture the castle, into which Simon escaped. Meanwhile Leicester had succeeded in crossing the Severn, and had marched as far as Evesham on his road to Kenilworth, hoping to join forces with his son. There he learnt of the younger Simon's misfortunes. Conscious that his last hour was come, the great Earl prepared with his handful of wornout and dispirited troops to sell his life dearly to the victorious Marchers.

The situation of Evesham with respect to the won is not altogether dissimilar to that of Lewes with respect to the Ouse. The river makes a great curve to the south, and Evesham is situated on the right bank towards the southern sweep of the reach. On 4th August the battle of Evesham was fought. Edward had taken the lesson of Lewes to heart, and had marshalled his superior forces with consummate prudence. He himself occupied in force the sort of isthmus formed by the windings of the won a little to the north of Evesham. This cut off Leicester's only retreat by land, while Gloucester, who was posted with the rest of the army on the left bank of the river beyond the town, cut off all possibility of escape over Evesham bridge. Leicester himself could not but admire his enemies' tactics. "By the arm of St. James," he swore, "they come on cunningly. Yet they have not taught themselves that order of battle, but have learnt it from me." The battle was short but sharp. Edward and Gloucester advanced simultaneously to the attack amidst a terrible blare of trumpets. Slowly but surely the little army of Leicester was surrounded and overwhelmed. Earl Simon died fighting bravely. At his side perished his first-born son Henry, the old playmate and companion-of-arms of the victor. Guy, the third son, was captured terribly wounded. The army of the good cause was annihilated, and Edward by one day of victory undid the efforts of seven years of struggle.

Henry III. was now restored to liberty, though it was, in truth, little more than a change of masters. Henceforth he was to act as the puppet of his son instead of his brother-in-law. But years and misfortunes had still further relaxed the will of the old king, and Edward was so careful to pay him due deference, so affectionate and devoted to him, that all trace of former jealousy was removed, and perfect harmony remained between father and son until the end of Henry's life. One more difficulty still stood in the way of a complete settlement. The wild thirst of the victors for vengeance forced the vanquished to fight till the bitter end. A general sentence of forfeiture drove the remnants of the baronial party to renew their resistance in the autumn. The dead Earl's stronghold of Kenilworth was the chief centre of the renewed struggle, but the younger Simon held out amidst the marshy fastnesses of the Isle of Axholme. By building long wooden bridges over the sluggish streams that cut off Axholme from the mainland, Edward procured in November his cousin's surrender. In the spring Edward won a great fight against the men of Winchelsea, which resulted in the surrender of the Cinque Ports. He then turned his arms against a famous freebooter, an outlawed knight named Adam Gurdon, who headed a band of desperadoes that lurked in the Hampshire forests on the pretext of

41

upholding to the last the good cause. Edward came upon Gurdon's camp in the neighbourhood of Alton. Thoroughly delighted with the adventure, he rushed impetuously forward, heedless of the fact that his followers had got separated from him by a deep ditch. He engaged in personal conflict with his doughty antagonist, and having wounded him, captured him after a sharp tussle, and, delighted with his bravery and daring, treated him with all honour, tending his wounds, and regarding him as his guest rather than his captured enemy. But the nonknightly followers of Adam were hanged on the nearest trees by Edward's orders. Meanwhile Kenilworth still held out. Its long resistance at last taught Edward that clemency was not only right but politic. After failing to storm the castle, Edward offered the "Disinherited "to restore them their lands on condition of their paying a fine amounting to five years' rental. The general acceptance of the terms of this "Dictum de Kenilworth "practically ended the English rising. But a few desperadoes, specially exempted from the pardon, still strove to hold the Isle of Ely as their fellows had previously held Axholme. They maintained their position so bravely that Edward was forced to go in person to the siege. By building causeways of wattles over the marshy fenland, he secured an access to the stronghold of the Disinherited. Treachery did something more. But clemency finally ended the struggle. Edward at last offered the enemy the terms of Kenilworth, whereupon they surrendered. This ended the war in England. But Llywelyn of Wales still stood out in the west, and as long as he was in arms the cause of the Montforts could not be said to be dead. But the papal legate

Ottobon, who had already done good work for peace, now offered his powerful intervention, which both Edward and Llywelyn hastened to accept. By the Treaty of Shrewsbury terms of exceptional liberality were offered to, and accepted by Llywelyn. In this treaty Henry recognised Llywelyn as prince of all Wales, and allowed him to receive the homage of all the Welsh barons save the degenerate representatives of the old line of princes of the south, who were still allowed the greater dignity of immediate vassals of the Crown. Edward's old territory of the Four Cantreds was fully surrendered to him, though this course left Edward nothing of his Welsh estates save the lands round Carmarthen. It was a great day of triumph for the Welsh national cause. It was also a great day of rejoicing to Edward, who thus by a noble surrender concluded his great work of peace and reconciliation. For the rest of the old king's reign the land remained in profound peace, thanks to the wise policy of Edward in identifying the monarchy with the more solid and permanent parts of the policy of the dead Earl of Leicester. In the nine years of struggle Edward's character had become matured and his experience ripened. He had already shown that he ranked among the first knights, generals, and statesmen of Christendom. Now that the swords of his followers were turned to ploughshares and their lances to reaping-hooks, Edward again went back to his old pastime of the tournament. But he soon resolved to consecrate to a higher purpose the sword which he had so often wielded against his kinsfolk and his countrymen, or in the savage sports of the tiltyard. In June 1268

Edward took the crusader's vow to rescue the sepulchre of Christ from the insults of Islam.

CHAPTER III

EDWARD AS A CRUSADER
1268-1272

THE great age of crusading had long passed away. It was no longer possible, as it had been two hundred years before, for a crusading prince to win with his sword a fair Eastern province. The Latin kingdom of Jerusalem had never recovered the deadly blows inflicted upon it by Saladin. The hosts of Islam had been long united, and opposed to the pious fury of the Christians as ardent a zeal, as devoted a bravery, and a far greater knowledge of the country and of the means of warfare appropriate to it. Yet the crusading impulse had by no means died away. All through the thirteenth century it remained the highest ideal of Christian knighthood to renounce all conflict with fellow Christians and fight the good fight of the Holy Cross against the blasphemous infidels who profaned the sepulchre of the Lord. The great Military Orders, whose establishments were scattered throughout Christendom, provided a constant stream of ardent and devoted recruits, and kept up a very necessary permanent element in the crusading forces. The greatest of the popes, the holiest of the saints, the mightiest of the kings of the greatest age of mediaeval Christendom were unwearied in their efforts to keep alive the holy war. But the growing complications of Western politics kept princes at home, though the constant degeneracy of the Eastern Christians necessitated a continual stream of new pilgrims if any effectual resistance were to be made to the ever increasing aggressions of Islam. The result was that the thirteenth-century Crusades assume a character of their own. They are no longer, as they once had been, the united effort of Western Europe. They are rather the results of individual piety and enterprise, a constant stream of petty expeditions rather than the occasional rush of a mighty army. They were seldom or never successful. All that the most ardent crusader could hope for was to discharge his personal vows or stay for a short time the advancing flood of Islam. There is then in the abortive Crusades of the age of Edward I. a higher and more exalted character than in the great military promenades of an earlier age. There was no longer the prospect of an Eastern kingdom to attract a selfish Bohemund, or the hopes of sharing in the spoils of a mighty empire to inspire the greed of the Venetian trader. It was purely a work of piety and self-sacrifice, tempered by love of adventure. Death, sickness, defeat were the common lot of the Eastern pilgrim. Yet the constant flow of crusaders never slackened for a day; and conscious of the futility of individual effort, the noblest minds of Christendom looked forward eagerly to the time when the great monarchs of Europe would again lay aside their feuds and unite with one accord in a pious effort to ransom the Holy Sepulchre. But the hoped-for moment never came, and as time rolled on, the crusading impulse, though still affecting exalted and adventurous souls, seemed to have lost its hold on the great masses of the people. It is significant that the Mendicant Orders, whose great

46

work among the poor gave them a grasp over reality which no other class possessed, had not, as a rule, the crusading fervour of the older religious bodies. Some, at least, of them saw that there was plenty of opportunity for pious enthusiasm at home. To relieve the daily miseries of the humble toilers at their own doors was a higher call upon men of religion than the pursuit of visionary ideals beyond sea. And with the growth of wider views of nature and religion that intense power possessed by the early Middle Ages of embodying its faith in concrete external acts became fainter. Many began to question whether piety might not be better employed than in the rough violence of crusading warfare. The religion of love was beginning to vie with the religion of war. The best and the worst of motives combined to slacken crusading enthusiasm.

France was now the greatest power in Christendom, and the best representative of the Christian ideals of the age. The Crusades had always been mainly a French movement, and now in their decline became more of a French movement than ever. The saintly hero who sat on the French throne was the only monarch in Christendom who had both the power and the will to lead a new great Crusade. In his early manhood St. Louis had failed miserably in his first Crusade in Egypt. He was now bent on consecrating his old age by a second crusading effort. At his command a Crusade was preached throughout Europe. It seemed as if the twelfth century had become renewed.

Edward was among the first to respond to the persistency of St. Louis. He had long been bound by the strongest ties of gratitude and affection to the great king who had come to his father's rescue in the extremity of his fortunes, and he was not unmindful of the tie of blood that bound him to the husband of his mother's sister. Edward's own strict religious training, his own exalted personal piety, bent him strongly in the same direction. It may even be that remorse for the violence of his youth may have contributed to induce him to direct the arms that had shed so much English blood against the infidel, to slay whom was a work of piety. His keen love of adventure was no longer satisfied with the violent distractions of the tiltyard. Anyhow he took the cross with enthusiasm, and with him the noblest and bravest of his countrymen assumed the sacred symbol. Unlike Edward, all did not fulfil their vow.

Edward took the cross in 1268, but two years more elapsed before he could start for the Holy Land. During this interval the zeal of the faithful was stirred up to undertake the Crusade by wandering preachers of the two great orders of friars. But there were still some troubles at home that delayed the departure of the crusaders; especially there was a struggle between Edward and the fierce and restless Gilbert of Gloucester, who declared that he would not go on Crusade and leave his estates exposed to the devastations of the Welsh. But the main difficulty in Edward's way was a financial one. The civil war had so exhausted the country that he found it impossible to collect the funds to fit out an expedition worthy of the cause and of his rank. His father was hopelessly involved in debt, and was in no condition to incur fresh liabilities. At last Edward was constrained to have recourse to St. Louis.

In return for a large advance, Edward pledged himself to follow the French king as Duke of Aquitaine, and submit himself and his followers to the jurisdiction of his uncle. At last, in August 1270, Edward set off from Dover, travelling first to Gascony, to set in order the affairs of his duchy, and thence through the rough hill country of Northern Spain to Aigues Mortes, near the mouth of the Rhone, whence St. Louis had already sailed on his Crusade. Among the French king's followers were his son Philip, and his brother Charles of Anjou, whom the favour of the pope had raised to that kingdom of Sicily, which Edward's brother Edmund had been too weak to retain. Edward was accompanied by his gallant cousin Henry of Almaine.

At Aigues Mortes Edward learnt that St. Louis had diverted his arms from Palestine to Tunis, and was encamped at Carthage engaged in a fierce struggle with the Mohammedan Sultan of Tunis, whose nearness to the kingdom of Sicily made him a dangerous neighbour to Charles of Anjou, if not to the Christian world at large. Edward sailed at once over the Mediterranean, but on his arrival he found that St. Louis had died of fever, and that his son, the new king, Philip the Hardy, had been led by his politic uncle, Charles of Anjou, to conclude a truce with the infidels. The sickness that raged throughout the camp was the pretext for this inglorious surrender, but though the chiefs approved of the politic step, the mass of the pilgrim host cried hotly against the worldliness of their leaders that had betrayed the good cause. Edward fully shared their indignation. "By God's blood," he swore, "though all my fellow-soldiers and countrymen desert me, I will go to Acre with

Fowin my groom, and keep my word and my oath to the death." Very reluctantly he bade his little fleet of thirteen ships set sail for Trapani in Sicily with the great French host. But the morning after their arrival off the Sicilian port a fearful storm arose. The fleet, anchored in the insecure roadstead of Trapani, suffered terribly. For three days the tempest raged. The crusaders' ships were driven from their anchorage and sunk like stones by the fury of the waves. Twenty-eight ships were destroyed. In one alone it was believed that a thousand pilgrims went down. But the hand of God protected Edward's little squadron. It was universally regarded as a divine sanction to Edward's indignation at the unworthy peace that not a single English ship was wrecked. A fortnight later King Philip left Trapani, taking with him in melancholy procession the corpses of his father and brother, to which were soon added the bodies of his wife and child. With him went Henry of Almaine, newly appointed as Edward's seneschal of Gascony. But a few weeks later Henry was brutally murdered by the reckless sons of Simon de Montfort, as he was praying in a church at Viterbo. All Christendom was terribly moved by the assassination. It showed that the fires of the civil war were not yet extinct.

Edward remained for the rest of the severe season at Trapani, whence he sailed in the early South Italian spring for the Holy Land. The Christian lordships in the Levant were reduced by this time to the slenderest proportions, though the old titles still remained to testify to the great empire that had been established by the first crusaders. There was still a nominal King of Jerusalem, an offshoot of that same house of

Lusignan with which Edward had been, through his grandmother's second marriage, so intimately connected. But Cyprus was the real centre of this power. On the mainland a few coast towns, conspicuous among which was the great city of Acre, alone paid obedience to the King of Jerusalem, while of the numerous great feudatories who had once supported the throne of the Godfreys and Baldwins, the united principality of Antioch and Tripoli alone remained, and had of late sustained a severe shock by the capture of Antioch in 1268 by the indefatigable Sultan Bibars, who, despite the constant threatenings of the vast swarms of Mongol barbarians from Central Asia, never lost an opportunity of turning his scimitar against the Christian colonists. But Acre even in the days of its ruin was no unworthy memorial of the great age of the Latin rule in the East. There was still centred the great trade between East and Westwhich the Crusades had opened up. There were still churches, palaces, castles, market-halls, storehouses, and huge walls of defence that bore vivid testimony to the greatness of the Latins as builders and architects. It was still one of the great towns of Christendom. The keen-eyed traders of Italy, the strenuous monastic soldiers of the great Military Orders, the fanatical and enthusiastic pilgrims, the lax and luxurious descendants of the original Frankish settlers, still jostled each other in its narrow and crowded streets. The strange contrasts of the Crusades, the superhuman virtue and the bestial vices, that alike found their representatives in the strange medley that followed the crusading host, were still brilliantly depicted in the daily life of its inhabitants. But Acre was still so strong that

Sultan Bibars stopped short in his career of conquest as he approached its walls, and turned his arms against Cyprus. Not till all the other outposts of Eastern Christendom were overthrown would he assail the strong and rich merchant city.

Edward on his voyage from Sicily first touched at Cyprus, and thence sailed direct to Acre. The English chroniclers who followed his fortunes exaggerate the difficulties of the city, and even suggest that it was closely besieged by the Sultan. But Bibars had ventured no farther than to attack and capture some of the neighbouring castles. No sooner had Edward arrived at Acre than a formidable attack of the Mongols on Northern Syria called away Bibars' army, while his fleet failed in their attack on Cyprus. Edward's little band inspired the men of Acre with a fresh enthusiasm. With the English prince at its head, the crusading army ventured on three forays, which penetrated deep into the heart of Mohammedan Palestine. But they were mere plundering expeditions, and had no great influence on the fortunes of the war. Moreover, the English died off like flies from the heat and from thirst, while others perished from their intemperate use of fruit, grapes, and honey. In the most successful of the forays Edward failed to capture a Saracen tower, and Bibars exultingly rejoiced that if the crusaders were not able with so large a force to secure a single castle, there was but little prospect of their conquering so great a territory as the kingdom of Jerusalem. At last the politic Charles of Anjou, the author of the truce at Tunis, sent messengers offering his mediation to bring about a peace. The Latin Christians of Syria eagerly welcomed their intervention, and their good offices induced Bibars to consent to a truce for ten years, which at least allowed Acre to carry on its commerce and rest awhile before the struggle was renewed. The truce was signed in April 1272, but Edward refused to be a party to it. As in the camp at Carthage, he would have no share with the unbeliever. He preferred to stand aside in proud and unreasonable isolation, while more practical politicians concluded the unworthy pact. His brother Edmund [since 1267 Earl of Lancaster], who had joined Edward at Acre, now hurried home to England, but Edward, always accompanied by the faithful Eleanor, still tarried in Syria, hoping against hope for fresh adventures.

The Sultan was disappointed at Edward's remaining at Acre, and did not scruple to send an assassin to seek his life. It was probably at Bibars' instigation that the Emir of Jaffa, one of the Sultan's great officials, now excited Edward's interest by professing an anxiety to become a Christian, and repeatedly sent to Acre an emissary, who could speak French, to treat with him on the matter. But the messenger was a satellite of the Old Man of the Mountain and versed in every diabolical art of the East. One hot evening in June 1272—it happened to be Edward's birthday—the envoy of the Emir approached his abode with an urgent message from his master. He was forthwith admitted into Edward's bedroom, and found the prince sitting on his bed, with uncovered head and clad only in a light tunic. The Mohammedan handed over a letter to Edward and bent low as he respectfully answered his questions. He put his hand to his belt as if to draw out another letter, but instead he quickly pulled out a poisoned dagger, which he aimed at Edward's heart. Edward was quick enough to ward off the blow with his arm, on which he received a deep wound. But he at once kicked down the assassin as he was threatening another blow. He then wrested the dagger from him and slew him with his own weapon. The attendants rushed in and found their master covered with blood and the murderer dead on the ground. The prince's minstrel dashed out the assassin's brains with a stool, and Edward rebuked him for striking a dead man. The Master of the Temple soon hurried in with precious drugs and smooth prophecies of recovery.

Next day Edward made his will. But after some days the flesh around the wounded arm grew black and threatening. The surgeons exchanged uneasy whispers, and sadness fell on every countenance. "What are you whispering about?" cried Edward. "Can I not be cured? Speak out and fear not." One of the doctors, an Englishman, answered, "You may be cured, but only at the price of intense suffering." Edward at once put himself in that surgeon's hands and bade him do all that he thought necessary. Thereupon the surgeon ordered Eleanor out of the room, and she was led away weeping and wailing. "It is better, lady," said the bystanders, "that you should weep than the whole of England." Next morning the same surgeon cut away all the blackened flesh from the prince's arm, consoling him with the promise that in fifteen days he would again be able to mount his horse. From that hour Edward rapidly recovered, though his constitution was permanently enfeebled, and many years later sharp attacks of sickness were traced back by his physicians to the effect of the assassin's blow. Sultan Bibars hardly believed that his enemy had escaped the well-planned assassination, but sent some of his chief counsellors to offer his congratulations. Edward received them civilly, but as they bowed low before him he said in English, "You pay me worship, but yet you love me not." But he prudently avoided making the treacherous act a pretext for renewing the war.

Alarming letters now reached Edward from home. Old King Henry wrote that his physicians despaired of prolonging his life, and urged his first-born to return home without delay. Accordingly Edward left Acre about the middle of August 1272, and after a voyage of seven weeks again landed at Trapani in Sicily, where he was magnificently entertained by his uncle, Charles of Anjou. But sad news now came from England. First came the tidings of the death of his elder son John, a bright and beautiful boy, whom he had left behind with his uncle King Richard. Then followed the intelligence of the death of the King of the Romans, and soon that of King Henry as well. But the news must also have come how on the old king's death King Edward had been peaceably proclaimed, and everywhere accepted with rejoicings. The long and weary years of probation were at last over, and Edward, at the age of thirty-three, had at last ascended the throne that he was so brilliantly qualified to adorn.

Fresh duties and responsibilities crowded upon the new king, but he never forgot that he had been a crusader, and never quite despaired of a new Crusade on a grander scale and with a happier result. A comrade of his pilgrimage at Acre, the holy and wise Archdeacon Theobald of Liège, had now been called to the papal throne. As he had bade farewell to Edward and his brother soldiers of the Cross, he had in the touching words of the Psalmist bound himself never to forget Jerusalem in her sorrows. On his way through Italy Edward visited his old friend and reported to him the sad condition of the Holy Land. Gregory X.—this was the name Theobald now assumed as pope—was not unmindful of his vows, and laboured with single-minded earnestness to appease the feuds of Christendom that all Christian people might unite in a holy war. The good pope saw his highest expectations realised when in 1274 he presided over a General Council at Lyons, which healed for a time the schism of the Eastern and Western churches, solemnly called Europe to arm against Islam, and imposed on the whole Western Church the obligation of devoting for six years a tenth of its revenues for the purposes of the Crusade. The Crusade was preached in every land in Christendom. In barbarous Finland and distant Iceland the wandering apostles of the Holy War pressed on their hearers to the sacred work. But the good pope died, and the fierce strife of faction again invaded the papal court. Neither would the princes of Europe set a term to their mutual jealousies to further the great work. Year after year the hope of a great Crusade became fainter. The crusading tenth was seized by temporal princes for temporal uses: even Edward did not scruple in his necessity to lay profane hands on the sacred treasure. The Latin Christians of the Holy Land saw with dismay that the stream of armed pilgrims fell off rather than grew. The unnatural union of Orthodox Greek and Catholic Latin soon broke asunder. At last the

Mohammedans swooped down upon their prey. In 1289 the fall of Tripoli completed the ruin of the northern principality of the Christians. In 1291 Acre itself succumbed after a fearful siege. With the fall of the great merchant city fell the last vestiges of the kingdom of Godfrey of Bouillon. Henceforth the crusaders' ambition was at best a pious wish, a hope that could not be satisfied. And the brightest visions of mediaeval Christendom became obscured when the Moslem ruled without a rival over the lands once hallowed by the sacred presence of the Redeemer.

CHAPTER IV

THE KING AND HIS WORK

WE have now followed with some minuteness the biography of Edward before his accession to the throne. No part of his life throws so great a light on his character and career, or illustrates more clearly the grounds on which we reckon Edward among the greatest of English statesmen. His long years of apprenticeship had not simply formed his character. They had also suggested the main lines of the policy on which he was to act for the whole of his long reign. It is not too much to say that every important aspect of Edward's work as king had been already foreshadowed in his work as a king's son. He had risen superior to his early failures in the field and in the council chamber. His first defeats had given him that power of adapting his tactics to circumstances which is his chief claim to be called a great commander. The Welsh policy suggested to him by his advisers when yet a mere boy contains in substance the Welsh policy of his reign. His early dealings with the fierce Llywelyn and his early efforts to make his Welsh lands shire-ground need only a slight development to become the policy which had its final outcome in the defeat and death of the Welsh prince and the annexation of the principality to the Crown. In the same way Edward's early experiences in Gascony suggested to him the whole of his subsequent policy for the consolidation and security of his Aquitainian possessions. Moreover, his constant dealings with the princes of Europe, most of them his near kinsfolk, cannot but have brought before his mind the main principles of that able and successful foreign policy which is one of the greatest results of his reign. And it is already a commonplace that the experience of the Barons' Wars substantially created the home policy of Edward's later life. To strengthen and develop the royal power; to widen the hold of the king on the nation by taking the people themselves into partnership with him in the administration of his inheritance; to work out under happier auspices the great ideas of Montfort, and to turn schemes meant to bring about a revolution into devices for the regular government of the realm; to stand forth, above all, as the truly national king, who ruled through the advice of his own nobles and scorned the foreign favourite and parasite—such were among the main lines of Edward's work as a king. Every detail almost of his constitutional policy had been already made clear to him during the life of his father. The lack of good laws during his father's days had impressed upon him the need of legislation, while the want of good government had made him realise the supreme importance of establishing sound administration. Thus it was, with plans already formed and ambitions already formulated, that Edward entered in 1272 into the great position of an English king. He was already resolved to make England supreme in Britain and England the mediator of Europe. He had already become a national constitutional ruler of a free and high-spirited people.

Thirty-three years of battling with the world had now formed both the body and mind of Edward. He looked every inch a king. The chroniclers speak with enthusiasm of the beauty and dignity of his person. He was a man of unusual and commanding height. Like another Saul, he overtopped most of his subjects by a head and shoulders. His frame was cast in a strong but elegant mould and was admirably proportioned. He had the long sinewy arms that make a good swordsman. His long lean legs, which won for him the popular nickname of Longshanks, gave him that firm grip over the saddle that makes the consummate horseman. All through his life he was as upright as a dart. His chest was broad and vaulted. Constant exercise and incessant activity kept down any disposition to corpulence, and down to his death he retained the slim regular proportions of his youth. His flowing hair shone in extreme youth like burnished silver. It gradually assumed a yellow tinge, and by the time he had reached manhood had attained a deep black colour, which again turned in old age to a snowy whiteness. He never showed any tendency to baldness, and the white hair of his age was as thick and abundant as the yellow tresses of his youth. His forehead was broad and high. His features were refined and regular. The only thing that marred their perfect beauty was a slight droop of the left eyelid, which he had inherited from his father. His dark eyes, soft and dovelike when he was at rest, shot forth fire like the eyes of a lion when he was moved to anger. They remained undimmed to extreme old age. His nose was large, well-shaped, and aquiline. His teeth remained strong and firm down to the day of his death. His complexion was dark, clear, and pale, and was thought to indicate his choleric temperament. His voice had a slight stammer in it, but when animated he could quite overcome this impediment, and speak with a simple and natural eloquence that often moved his susceptible auditors to tears.

Edward's character was cast in a grand and simple mould. His general instincts were high-minded, noble, and generous. Like most mediaeval heroes, he was a man of strong emotions, and the rough wear and tear of a long life did not destroy, though perhaps they deadened, the deep affections and the loving heart half hidden by his pride and passion. He was the best of sons, fathers, and husbands. He was the most faithful and generous of friends. His chief fault in those relations was his slowness to see anything blameworthy in those whom he loved, or even in those who had rendered him useful service. His private life was absolutely pure and without reproach. His public action, always able, was, with a few exceptions, strictly upright and honourable. He had almost a passion for truth and justice, and it was not for nothing that "keep troth" was inscribed upon his tomb.

A character so strong, a will so firm as Edward's could not be without its faults. Many of these proceeded from the extraordinary impetuosity and violence which lay at the bottom of Edward's temperament. This disposition accounts for a good deal of the wanton and brutal violence of the doings which so scandalised right-thinking men in his extreme youth. It accounts for many of those grave defects of character brought out with such uncompromising clearness and precision by the nameless partisan of Simon de Montfort, who wrote that Song of Lewes which best explains to us the standpoint of the baronial party. To this hostile writer Edward was "a lion in pride and fierceness, not slow in attacking the strongest places, and fearing the onslaught of no man." But there was a less noble side to his character. He was, says the songwriter, "a panther in inconstancy and changeableness." "When he is in a strait he promises whatever you wish, but as soon as he escapes he repudiates his promise." In this respect Edward never quite got the better of the evil tendencies of his youth. The violation of his oath after the capture of Gloucester in 1264 is too faithfully paralleled by the treacherous way in which, a few years before his death, he obtained papal absolution from his oath to observe Magna Carta and the Forest Charter as enlarged and developed in 1297. Moreover, Edward was always excessively rash, impulsive, hot-headed, passionate, and even vindictive. Yet a humble submission or the frank acknowledgment of an offence at once mollified him, however furious was his wrath. One day when he was a young man he was hawking on the banks of a certain river. One of his companions, posted on the other bank of the stream to that occupied by Edward, blunderingly let free a hawk, which had seized a wild duck amidst the osier-beds. Edward grew angry, abused and threatened his follower. But the careless falconer, seeing that neither bridge nor ford was near, answered impudently, "It is well for me that the river divides us." Edward burst into a furious rage, plunged with his horse into the unknown depths of the stream, and having successfully crossed over, climbed with difficulty up the steep bank hollowed out by the action of the water. The luckless follower fled in terror, but Edward pursued him with drawn sword, and soon caught him up. But his anger was at once ended when the man uncovered his head and knelt humbly to implore his master's forgiveness. Edward put back his sword in the scabbard, and soon lord and follower were back at the river bank seeking with the utmost harmony to bring back the strayed hawk. Many years later Edward was moved to anger by the clumsiness of one of the squires attending him on the occasion of the marriage of his daughter Margaret. He seized a stick and soundly belaboured the unlucky squire with it, inflicting on him such injury that, when the fit of temper was over, he heartily repented of his violence and sought to heal his servant's wounds by a present of the very considerable sum of £13:6:8.

Edward hated his enemies quite as heartily as he loved his friends, and liked power so well that he grew quite mad at the least opposition or contradiction. He was always terribly in earnest, and being quite convinced of the honour and integrity of his own ends, was always ready to impute unworthy motives to his opponents, and was, in fact, opposed so unscrupulously that he often had good reason for his worst suspicions. Edward also possessed that strange power, often found in temperaments like his, of persuading himself that what he desired was right, and that the means which he selected to attain a good end were necessarily consecrated by the excellence of his object. "The wiles or tricks," sang the partisan critic of his youth, "by which he is advanced, he calls prudence, and the way whereby he attains his end, crooked though it be, seems to him straight and open. Whatever he likes he says is lawful, and he thinks that he is released from the law, as though he were greater than the king." Edward was never a very reflective or thoughtful man. Like many great men of action, he took the course that seemed to him the most likely to lead him straight to his end, and did not ponder too much over its lawfulness. But so far as he pondered over his courses at all, he sought honestly to live according to the law, and there have been few prophecies more signally falsified than that of the writer of the Song of Lewes, who foretold that Edward's reign would be a most miserable one for England, inasmuch as his wish was to be a king above the law. Edward was proud of his high standard of honour and truthfulness, and as compared with his contemporaries, his boast is in no wise a vain one. But if those who saw in Edward a lawless self-seeker were but blind judges, still more have those erred who saw in him a cold-blooded, calculating, and scheming lawyer, heedless of justice so long as he could get formal right on his side. It is not in such ways that the right clue can be attained for the appreciation of his ardent and impetuous character. Edward was very conscious of his royal dignity, and proud and ambitious to no ordinary degree. But there was little that was mean or sordid even in the lowest of his ambitions. The aristocratic contempt for men of mean birth and humble station, which had been so unpleasant a feature of his early manhood, he almost outlived; though at times of danger and difficulty, when the Welsh troops showed signs of mutiny before Falkirk, or when the weavers of Ghent, rising against the oppressions of his soldiers, threatened his

64

very life, it flashed forth again with something of its old insolence and scorn. But there was very little in Edward of that miserable class feeling that was so unlovely a feature among the knights and gentlemen that supported the court of his grandson. Edward loved his people, and possessed many popular qualities that endeared him to them. Though constantly beset by troubles and difficulties, he seldom lost his cheerfulness, except to sorrow for the loss of those dear to him. Down to an advanced age he joined in the rough and not very refined practical jokes and merriments of mediaeval society. One Easter Monday he suffered five ladies of the court to make him their mock prisoner, and bought his redemption by a liberal present to his captors. Nor was he less gracious to his followers of low degree. One day in a merry mood, as he was setting out for the hunt, he gave his horse to his washerwoman, Matilda of Waltham, on the condition of her riding a race on the king's hunter and defeating the other competitors. His ready eloquence was in itself a means of delighting his people. No less commendable were his earnestness and indefatigability at the seat of judgment. He delighted in unravelling a knotty point of law, and prided himself upon his zeal for the poor and oppressed. He gloried in his reputation for clemency. He really sought to identify himself with every rank of his people, and this great endeavour made him a thoroughly national king.

Edward had the good luck to pass through a sterner discipline and a stricter apprenticeship than commonly falls to the lot of those called to ascend an hereditary throne. He thus learnt to put a curb upon his feelings, and repress the first rush of his angry passions in a way that speaks most strongly for the strength of his character and the nobleness of his aims. His self-restraint in his middle life was, for such a man, admirable. As misfortunes gathered around him he became less able to conceal or check his emotions; but down to the last he withstood opposition that might well have ruined the temper of a calmer and milder man. Not only had he to face the opposition of large sections of his subjects, and the enmity of powerful kings and nations—his private affairs were always made miserable by the millstone of debt which hung round his neck from his first entrance into public life, and from which he could never free himself down to his dying day. The burden which Edward had inherited from his father was sufficiently overwhelming. He increased it by the obligations which he had been forced to incur during his Crusade. When he came to the throne he found himself hopelessly in the hands of the greedy companies of Lombard bankers, who had begun to push themselves into the position which had hitherto been monopolised by Jewish usurers. In after years Edward formed so many great designs that he was always more and more in want of money. From this perpetual indebtedness sprang half the defects of Edward's character, and more than half of the difficulties of his reign. Edward's poverty accounts for his troubles with the Londoners, his eagerness to open up new taxes, and the ever increasing discontent of his subjects. He handed on the burden to his son, and the weight which the great father had hardly been able to bear proved too overwhelming for his weak and incompetent successor.

The limited character of Edward's means made necessary a life of the utmost frugality and sobriety. Edward's own personal tastes drew him strongly in the same direction. He was always rigidly economical, and even upon occasions parsimonious. But on state occasions his hospitality was truly regal, and he found enough money to keep up a good stud of horses, though he was ever lavish in giving them away to his friends and kinsfolk. He was particularly bountiful to poor knights, feeling the full force of the strong tie which bound the knighthood of Christendom together in a single brotherhood of equals. The simplicity of his attire suggested the simplicity of his daily life. After his coronation Edward never once wore his crown, thinking that the dignity which it gave to his royal state was more than counterbalanced by the heaviness of the great bauble. He wore the plainest clothes. He did not affect the royal purple, but, like a common man, was clad in a plain short-sleeved tunic bordered with fur, and all of the same colour. One day he was asked by a hermit why he affected such ordinary garb. "I should not be a better man," answered Edward, "however splendidly I was dressed." The same simplicity was manifested in all his habits of life; but for all that Edward was keenly conscious of his royal dignity, and there were few who could venture to presume upon his easy familiarity. His court was very free from the luxury and extravagance which are the besetting sins of courts. Though many of Edward's followers were vicious and corrupt men, they were with hardly an exception hard workers and earnest politicians.

The tournament in early life, hunting and hawking until the end of his career, were Edward's favourite diversions. As a sportsman his special delight was in chasing down deer on horseback, and, on catching them up, slaughtering them with his sword. His strong love of the chase made him as jealous as the Norman kings in keeping up his forests and maintaining the forest laws in their old oppressive rigour. His constant indulgence in field sports and manly exercises secured him splendid health, though his infancy had been sickly and though his wound in the Holy Land gave him trouble for many years. The same careful way of life, combined with strict frugality and temperance, secured for Edward a green old age. He had attained what in the Middle Ages was the very advanced age of sixty-seven before there were any signs of his constitution breaking down.

Edward was deeply and unaffectedly religious. His piety was shown not only in his assiduity in attendance at mass and in his zeal in going on pilgrimages, but in his large and unostentatious charities (all the more creditable when we remember his chronic state of debt), and in the whole tone and tenor of his daily life. Straitened as were his resources, Edward was able to make grants to the two English universities, to the Knights of St. John, and to many famous monasteries, such as Durham, Glastonbury, Westminster, and St. Alban's. He was the refounder of the Cistercian abbey of Conway, when the needs of his Welsh policy involved the absorption of the old home of the monks in his new castle and fortifications. He contributed largely towards the cost of the new church and buildings erected by the monks on the opposite bank of the Conway river at Meynam. But his great work as a monastic patron was the foundation of the Cistercian abbey of Vale Royal, in a deep and secluded hollow of the valley of the Weaver, in the very heart of his own earldom of Chester. This pious undertaking Edward began in 1266, in fulfilment of a vow which he had made when exposed to great peril of shipwreck; but lack of means made the progress of the work slow, and it was not until 1277 that the monks were able to enter into the full possession of their founder's bounty. But while Edward thus practically showed his sympathy for the older religious orders, he was, like most men of his age, strongly under the influence of the mendicant friars. His confessors were generally Dominicans, but the Franciscans, in whose great church in London he treasured up the heart of his beloved Eleanor, were also largely in his confidence.

Like a good Englishman, Edward reverenced most of all saints of English birth, such as St. John of Beverley, to whose shrine he was never weary of making pilgrimages, and above all, St. Edward the Confessor, his namesake and predecessor. His religion was of that half-martial kind which is so characteristic of the early Middle Ages, but which was already becoming more rare owing to the new types of spiritual perfection held up by the saints among the Mendicant Orders. This element gave a reality and fervidness to Edward's constant aspirations after a Crusade. What in the mouth of Philip the Fair or Clement V. was the merest hypocrisy or conventionality, was to Edward an honest and sincere recognition of the clear ideal of the duty of a

Christian knight. And Edward was all too ready to read his crusading ambitions into his everyday wars. Llywelyn or Robert Bruce were to him men accursed by Holy Church, and he saw too readily a high religious impulse in what was largely the prompting of his own ambition and revenge. But a respect for ecclesiastical authority, which hampered his dealings with popes and archbishops, was at least a very real thing. Not even the barefaced partisanship of a series of fiercely Guelfic popes, not even the persistent and wearing opposition which Edward's own prelates so constantly offered to his policy, could quite eradicate from Edward's mind the deep lessons of respect for the authority of the Holy See and the spiritual independence of the English episcopate which had been so firmly ingrained into his mind in youth. But Edward, with all his spirit of reverence, was singularly free from the grosser superstitions of his time. On one occasion a beggar pretended that his sight had been restored through his prayers at the tomb of Henry III., and Queen Eleanor of Provence was delighted that this miracle attested her dead husband's claim to sanctity. But Edward drove the beggar away in anger, saying, "My father would rather have had such a lying knave blinded than have given him back his sight." Edward piously saw in all the many hairbreadth escapes of his adventurous life the direct finger of Providence, and, with something of a fatalist's contempt of danger, exposed himself to the worst risks of battle and siege. When his horse was shot by a missile from Stirling Castle, his followers begged him to withdraw from the range of its walls. But Edward answered in Biblical phrase, "A thousand shall fall

70

beside me, and ten thousand at my right hand, but their arrows shall not come nigh unto me to do me hurt, for the Lord is with me." One day in his youth he was playing chess with a certain knight in a vaulted chamber. Without any particular reason, he arose from his seat and went to the other end of the room. Thereupon a huge stone crashed down from the roof, destroying the chair on which Edward had been sitting. He attributed his preservation to Our Lady of Walsingham, whom he held ever afterwards in special honour.

Edward was pre-eminently a man of action, but he was by no means altogether lacking in intellectual and artistic tastes. He certainly had a familiar knowledge of English, French, and Latin. Possibly he also knew Spanish, in which tongue he sometimes corresponded with his brother-in-law Alfonso of Castile. He was no great lover of books and no very bountiful patron of men of letters; yet he seems to have had some taste for the romances of chivalry, delighting in the legends of knights and paladins, in histories of such as those of Tancred the Crusader, in devotional treatises, and in books on agriculture. It was from a manuscript belonging to Edward at the time of his Crusade, that Rustician of Pisa made his well-known abridgment of the vast cycle of Breton romances, a work which attained a great success, and which, translated into Italian, afforded the material for a large number of poems. Nor should Edward's interest in English history be forgotten, or his care for the safe preservation of the national archives under proper custody. He was much more a patron of art than of letters, showing a particular taste for richly decorated sculpture, as seen in the crosses

71

commemorating Queen Eleanor, and perhaps still better in the exquisite statuary on the magnificent tombs of his father, wife, and brother in Westminster Abbey, the work apparently of an Italian artist. He completed his father's rebuilding of Westminster, but lack of means prevented his indulging in the expensive taste of building on a large scale. He was also fond of music, supplementing his English trumpeters and harpers with German fiddlers, and rejoicing, even in his hostile progresses in Scotland, when seven women met him on the wayside, and sang before him the songs of their country, as they had been wont to do in the days of King Alexander.

There is no need to expatiate upon Edward's claims to statesmanship. Contemporaries compared him to Henry II., and certainly no other one of our earlier kings can be rightly put in the same high place as Edward. But though there is a real relation between the work of Henry and that of Edward, and though Henry was perhaps the greater and more original mind of the two, yet Edward's task was complicated by difficulties of a subtle kind to which Henry had been a complete stranger. It was Edward's difficult task to adjust the despotism which Henry had set up to meet the national aspirations after liberty, and the popular cry to control the state which in the twelfth century had not yet arisen. That Edward abundantly succeeded in his difficult task will be sufficiently clear in nearly every page of the history of his reign. Without any great originality of character, without that insight and foresight which genius alone can give, Edward was able to apply to the great problems of statecraft an intellect of a high order, clear, logical, orderly, and decisive. But his character was stronger than his intellect, and his tenacity of purpose and pertinacity in conduct were seldom excelled by the excitable kings and statesmen of the Middle Ages. It is a commonplace to dwell on the legislative mind of Edward. But it is a very superficial view of the great king's character that regards him simply as a mere lawyer, even a great lawyer like his friend Bishop Burnell. It would be truer to say that Edward's chief merit as a legislator is that he knew how to follow the lines laid down by his ministers and judges. The statute-book tells us nothing of motives and springs of conduct, but it is hard not to believe that the main merit of Edward's work as a lawgiver belongs to his advisers. Theirs at least was the initiative. It is merit enough in a born king that he knew whose advice to follow and in what direction he was to go. The personal characteristics of Edward come out even more in his statecraft and his generalship than in his legislation.

As a soldier Edward's character is perhaps most completely seen. He was the true knight of chivalry, brave to recklessness, careless of his life, careless of all ulterior consequences, throwing his whole soul into the fierce rush of the feudal charge which scattered the Londoners at Lewes, or wrestling hand to hand in long and doubtful struggle with the fierce Adam Gurdon or the treacherous Count of Châlon. But with increasing experience the knightly hero grew into a real general. The same power of self-restraint, which marks every side of Edward's character, enabled him to curb the rash valour which he had learnt in the tourney and tilt-yard, and aspire to a degree of tactical and strategic skill rare indeed in the age in which he lived. His greatest military qualities were his capacity of profiting by adverse experience, and his rare skill in varying his method of warfare to meet the tactics adopted by the enemy. In his continental campaigns, Edward remained to the end a mere captain of feudal chivalry. But he very clearly realised that there were times and places where the heavily armed mounted knight was of little military value. His early defeats by the light-armed and nimble Welsh footmen taught him the value of a dexterous and daring irregular infantry, and suggested to him that policy of carrying on Welsh warfare like a great siege, which proved so irresistible in 1277 and 1282. Moreover, Edward paid a high tribute to the conquered Welsh in the large use which he made of them in all his subsequent campaigns, and notably in the wars in Scotland and Flanders. In the same way Edward had the quickness and the skill to borrow from Montfort the tactics that had proved fatal to his own and his father's cause at Lewes, and, bettering his lesson, he turned his uncle's teaching against him in his cleverly won victory at Evesham. In his old age Edward was not too proud to learn another lesson. He had the eyes to discern that the close array of the Scottish infantry at Falkirk could not be broken by the mere rush of a cavalry charge. He won the crowning victory of his life by his skilful employment of archers to break up the squares of the Scots with their missiles. His combination of the heavy cavalry of England with the light infantry and archers of Wales prepared the way for the more complete working out of this system which resulted from the famous English victories during the Hundred

Years' War with France. The two chief lines of military progress in subsequent generations lay in the development of a trained force of infantry and in the increase of the efficiency of the bowman. In both these respects Edward is a forerunner, though perhaps a half-blind one, of the improvements in the art of war which marked the next two centuries.

The great men of the thirteenth century embody the best ideals of the Middle Ages, but there is also something modern in their character and ambitions. Edward himself partakes of this twofold nature. As a man he seems almost purely mediaeval. Yet as an English statesman he could conceive the idea of a national state ruled by a strong king, but controlled by a popular Parliament. As a diplomatist he could grasp the conception of a European equilibrium, to be maintained by a judicious policy of mediation on the part of his island kingdom. As a British patriot he longed for the time when England, Scotland, Wales, and Ireland were all parts of the same kingdom. As a warrior he dimly foreshadowed the battle array of Crecy or Agincourt. And many-sided as was his activity, there was a perfect balance and harmony between the various elements of his policy. His eulogisers and detractors have, as a rule, fixed on some one side of his policy, and confined their praise or blame to that side alone. It is only when we take in his character as a whole, that we can fully realise how real are his claims to be regarded as a "greatest of the Plantagenets." No rulers of England save William the Conqueror, Henry II., Henry VIII., and Cromwell, can be compared with him, either as regards force of character and strength of intellect, or as regards the greatness and the permanence of their influence on the history of our land.

Edward's family and court next demand our attention. He was strongly amenable to domestic influence, and the weak and tender sides of his father's character continued to have an influence for good over him many years after experience had taught him the folly and evil of his father's policy. His mother, Eleanor of Provence, continued to have a strong hold over him until her death in 1291. His close affection and devotion to his first wife, Eleanor of Castile, need not be further dwelt upon. He was warmly attached to his sister Margaret, the wife of Alexander III. of Scotland, and his care for the welfare of his nephew, John of Brittany, is the best proof that Edward was equally devoted to his other sister Beatrice, the wife of the Duke of Brittany. Edward's only brother, Edmund, Earl of Lancaster, was not quite the man to exercise a strong influence over any one; but Edward's care for his brother's interests is seen in the vast estates which gradually accumulated round the founder of the greatest baronial house of mediaeval England, and in the trust with which he allowed Edmund to manage his diplomacy and lead his armies at the most critical period of his reign. Edmund himself was Earl of Lancaster and Leicester and Derby, receiving after Evesham the confiscated titles and estates of Simon de Montfort and Robert Ferrers. By arranging the marriage of Edmund's heir, Thomas, with the heiress of his most trusted follower, Henry Lacy, the Earl of Lincoln, Edward still further increased the greatness of the Lancastrian house, and made possible that extraordinary combination of power which Earl Thomas, as the head of the Lords Ordainers, was able to bring to bear against Edward II. Nor was Edward inattentive to his more distant kinsfolk. His uncle Richard, King of the Romans, had a real influence over him. He was devotedly attached to Richard's eldest son, his cousin, Henry of Almaine, and strove hard to avenge his tragic death. Richard's younger son and successor, Earl Edmund of Cornwall, had always a high place in his cousin's affections and counsels.

Edward was the father of a large family, though but few of his children attained manhood, and only three reached middle life. By Eleanor he had thirteen children, four sons and nine daughters. But of the four sons, the two eldest, John (1266-1272) and Henry (died 1274), both died in early boyhood. Alfonso, the third son, born in 1273 at Bayonne, died in 1284, a few months after the birth of his youngest brother, Edward of Carnarvon (born 1284), less fortunate in his unglorious life than his brothers in their early graves. Of Eleanor's nine daughters, four died as children. Of those that survived the eldest was Eleanor, born in 1264, and married to the Count of Bar in 1293. She died in her thirty-fifth year. The next was Joan of Acre, born in 1272 during her father's Crusade, and destined in her childhood to be the bride of Hartmann, the son of Rudolf of Hapsburg. She was married in 1290 to Earl Gilbert of Gloucester, Edward's old ally in the struggle against Montfort, who was nearly thirty years older than herself. After Gloucester's death, in 1295, Joan gave herself to the simple knight, Ralph of Monthermer. Edward was very angry at his daughter's disparagement, and threw Ralph into prison; but Joan defended herself with great spirit and energy, and her father, who loved his children, soon relented, and finally gave his low-born son-in-law the custody of the great Gloucester inheritance. She died in the same year as her father, transmitting to her son, the young Earl Gilbert, who died so gallantly on the field **of Bannockburn, some** spark of her father's great spirit. The next daughter, Margaret (1275-1318), married Duke John of Brabant in 1290, and lived to the then respectable age of forty-three. Mary, the fourth daughter, born in 1279, was doomed from early childhood to take the veil at Amesbury to please her grandmother, Eleanor of Provence, who ended her life in semi-monastic retirement in that famous convent. Edward was unwilling to sacrifice the child, but yielded to his mother's pressure. She attained at least her fifty-fourth year, an age far greater than that reached by her brothers and sisters. The youngest daughter, Elizabeth, surnamed the Welshwoman, born at Rhuddlan in 1282, was married first to John, Count of Holland (1297), and secondly to Humphrey, Earl of Hereford (1302). She died in 1316. Eleanor of Castile died in 1290, and after nine years of solitude Edward married a second time in 1299. But his second marriage was partly at least the result of political calculations; and Edward's second queen, Margaret of France, the sister of Philip the Fair, is a far more shadowy figure in our history than the gracious Eleanor of Castile. She is vaguely described as a "fair and marvellously virtuous lady." A girl of eighteen married to an old man of sixty could never stand in the place of the faithful partner of Edward's youth. She bore Edward three children.

The eldest, Thomas, born at Brotherton in Yorkshire in 1300, became Earl of Norfolk, and died in 1338. The second, Edmund, was born at Woodstock in 1301, and was made Earl of Kent. His unlucky end in 1330 is one of the worst stains on the regency of Mortimer and Isabella on behalf of the young Edward III. The third child of the second marriage was a daughter named Eleanor, born in 1306, who died when quite a child.

Edward's plans for the settlement of his family are of great historical importance. The younger sons he provided for with English earldoms, while the daughters were married to foreign princes whose alliance was of importance, or to great English earls, that their tendency to join the opposition ranks might be counterbalanced by their close personal connection with the royal house. In this respect Edward's policy anticipates that of Edward III. But like the more famous family settlement of Edward III. it was something of a failure.

Edward's ministers fill a large part in the history of his reign; though the scanty chronicles and the bare and formal legal records, from which we get most of our information, make it hard for us to assign to the king and his helpers their due share of merit, and render it almost impossible for us to get any very clear notion of the personal characteristics of even the greatest statesmen that stood round Edward's throne.

Edward's own kinsfolk take a considerable position among his counsellors. His brother Edmund of Lancaster, his representative in Guienne; his cousin Edmund of Cornwall, the regent during his long absence between 1286 and 1289; his nephew John of Brittany, his faithful vicegerent during the most critical period of his dealings with Scotland, all served Edward with the utmost loyalty, and were entirely trusted by him. Even the foreign relatives, who after the storms of the Barons' Wars scarcely dared to show their faces in England, still continued to enjoy Edward's confidence abroad. All through his reign, the Lusignans helped him in Gascony. His cousin, Count Amadeus the Great of Savoy, rendered him most important assistance in his later foreign policy. From that same Savoyard land came John de Grailly, the faithful seneschal of Aquitaine, and Otho of Grandison, or Grandson, who came from the town famous in after ages for the crushing defeat of Charles the Bold by the Swiss confederates, and who was a very important figure in the diplomatic history of the latter part of Edward's reign.

At home Edward's chief ministers were Englishmen, for the most part ecclesiastics, and though of gentle birth they but seldom belonged to the highest orders of society. Foremost amongst them is Robert Burnell, the Shropshire squire's son, who became the most dexterous of Chancery lawyers, and who, attaching himself to Edward when he was still but Earl of Chester and Duke of Aquitaine, remained united to him by the closest ties of personal friendship and harmony of policy until his death in 1292. Edward loved Burnell so well that he strove, even before his father's death, to make him Archbishop of Canterbury, and as soon as he became king secured for him the chancellorship and the bishopric of Bath and Wells. Burnell was undoubtedly a consummate lawyer, a skilful diplomatist, and a thoroughly faithful minister; but his private character was stained by licentiousness and greed, that stand in strong contrast to the purity and economy of the king. Even his wonderful munificence did not make Burnell popular; yet there is no single minister of whom we can say more clearly that he was a necessary element in the greatness of the reign. He probably deserves the largest share of the credit of the great legislative achievements of Edward I.

Burnell is the highest type of Edward's lawyer-statesmen. Next to him comes John Kirkby, Bishop of Ely, the subtle financier, to whose doings we shall often again have occasion to refer. Judges like Hengham and Britton, and civilians like the Italian legist Francesco Accursi—of whom we shall speak later—filled a subordinate position in Edward's court, and while giving technical details and scientific form to their master's work, had no great share in determining its spirit. After Burnell, the three leading ministers of Edward were Henry Lacy, Earl of Lincoln, Anthony Bek, Bishop of Durham, and Walter Langton, Bishop of Lichfield. Henry Lacy, Earl of Lincoln, was the only one of the great earls who remained unswervingly faithful to Edward, and who, despite his great name and vast estates, never shirked labour or trouble in the service of his master. He was courteous, handsome, and active, as brave in war as ripe in counsel. He fought for Edward's cause, both as a general and as a diplomatist. In Wales, Scotland, and France we find constant traces of his activity. When Edward became king, Lincoln had but barely attained his majority. Until his death in 1311, he never faltered in his allegiance; his regard for the father leading him to give what support he could to Edward II., even when the young king most flagrantly went against his father's policy. Unfortunate in his domestic life, Lincoln lost his two sons by violent deaths; and by the surrender of his two earldoms of Lincoln and Salisbury to his daughter Alice, whom Edward married to his own nephew Thomas of Lancaster, the old earl handed over to the royal house the great estates, which all through his life had been devoted to the loyal service of the Crown.

Anthony Bek, Bishop of Durham, is another striking figure among Edward's ministers. The son of a wealthy Lincolnshire lord, he was elevated when still a young man to the great palatine see of Durham. His love of pomp, luxury, and munificence well became the holder of one of the greatest posts in the Church, and one who was also secular lord of the rich county of Durham, which he ruled as freely with his crosier as Edward ruled his own patrimony of Chester by his sword. Bek's attitude to politics, like that of the Earl of Lincoln, was essentially that of a great magnate; but he was for many years as faithful as Burnell himself in his devotion to the royal service, and honourably distinguished from the Bishop of Bath by the purity of his private life. Yet Bek was a soldier and a statesman rather than a bishop, and never shone to greater advantage than when, at the head of his knights, he did good service for his master in the campaigns against the Scots, or when, at the head of a pompous embassy, he built up a close alliance between Edward and Adolf, King of the Romans. But Bek never forgot that he was a great prelate, and towards the end of the reign he joined the clerical opposition and forfeited the favour of the king. His elder brother, Thomas Bek, Bishop of St. David's, was also a prelate of great importance during this reign, doing nearly as much for the king in Wales as Anthony a few years later did for the king in Scotland.

Walter Langton is as much the minister of the end of Edward's reign as Burnell is the statesman of its earlier years. He began life as a poor man, became a clerk of the king's Chancery, and after Burnell's death drifted gradually into the position of Edward's chief adviser. In 1295 he was made treasurer, and in 1296 Bishop of Lichfield. He kept the treasury until Edward's death. Like that of Burnell, his private character was not beyond reproach; but, like Burnell, he served his master with unswerving fidelity. He shared very largely in the unpopularity which Edward contracted in the later violent years of his reign, and was made the scapegoat of his master's policy after the old king's death.

Edward's chief ministers were of exemplary fidelity, but one of the king's constant difficulties was with his subordinate agents, whose violence and greed often defeated the king's best laid schemes and involved their master in odium that though natural was hardly deserved. Even the lawyers required the constant eye of the master to keep them in order. During Edward's long absence abroad, between 1286 and 1289, the royal officials committed so many misdeeds that the king on his return was obliged to make a stern example. He almost cleared out the judicial bench of the greedy and venal judges, who, with Hengham at their head, had wrested the law to make their own fortune. Even less satisfactory were the ruffianly bailiffs and sheriffs, whose misrule gave the lie to Edward's policy of sound government and equal justice in Wales. More hated still were the close-fisted Italian merchants who farmed the king's revenue, and whose expulsion from the realm was one of the chief demands made by the people, when Edward's death brought about a new period of weak rule. But in no mediaeval country were things any better than in the England of Edward I. Even the trained clerks and knights of the French royal household conceived that their devotion to the king privileged them to commit any acts of violence they thought fit among his subjects.

Such was the king, his family, and his court. Called to the throne in 1272, Edward first set foot in England in 1274. The first half of his reign saw him mainly occupied with the reduction of North Wales and the carrying out of a great series of legislative changes. He was also very busy with his elaborate and successful foreign policy; to which, after the settlement of Wales, he was able to devote a more exclusive attention. Hence his long absence from England from 1286 to 1289. His return was followed by the last great memorials of his legislation.

The second period of Edward's reign begins about 1290. His chief occupation was now the attempted conquest and settlement of Scotland, a task complicated by rebellion in Wales and by the vigorous attack of Philip the Fair on Gascony. Moreover, Edward was now confronted by a revival of the baronial opposition, which forced upon him constitutional changes, whose completion is one of the greatest results of the second half of his reign. A fresh trouble arose from the clerical opposition, that, already troublesome in Edward's earlier years, now came to a head. The result tried the king's severest energies, but he never succumbed to his difficulties, and though he died with his work all undone, he left the impress of his mind and action on every branch of the national life.

It is now our task to go over in more detail the history thus outlined in brief. For the first period of the reign it will be most convenient to take each aspect of Edward's policy separately, and devote distinct chapters to his foreign policy, his Welsh policy, his legislation, his dealings with the estates and the working out of the parliamentary system, and the beginnings of his troubles in Scotland. After 1292 another course will be advisable. The complex troubles which now beset the king can only be fully realised if we follow a more chronological method, and see year by year how Edward's dealings with Scotland, France, the baronage, and the Church were all woven together in one inextricable whole and acted and reacted upon each other. When both sides of our task are done we shall be in a better position to measure his claims to be a great English statesman.

CHAPTER V

EDWARD'S CONTINENTAL POLICY
1272-1289

EDWARD had first learnt his accession to the throne in Sicily. In February 1273 he bade adieu to Pope Gregory at Orvieto and began his slow journey homewards. He was already a man of no small mark, and wherever he went he received a most flattering reception. As he passed through Lombardy in great pomp the people flocked out to meet him with the cry, "Long live the Emperor Edward." The doctors of Padua made him a member of the legal faculty of their famous university. The Milanese presented him with horses richly caparisoned with scarlet. He formed friendships with princes and cities that in after years stood him in good stead. He finally traversed the lands of his great-uncle, the aged Count Philip of Savoy, crossing the Mont Cenis early in June, and forcing a petty lord of the kingdom of Aries to perform homage to him as a punishment for plundering the baggage of the English on their way to the Crusade. Once beyond the Alps, Edward was joined by a large number of English magnates, so that he entered French territory at the head of a little army of more than a thousand lances. The boastful nobles of France had grown envious of Edward's fame as a warrior, and the Count of Châlon on the Saone, a vassal of the Duke of Burgundy, challenged him to a passage of arms. The tournament was fought out with such desperate earnestness that it became plain that the French wished for something other than a mere chivalrous display. The Count and Edward fought fiercely against each other with swords; until the Count, despairing of finding a weak place in his enemy's harness, flung his arms heavily around the king's neck and sought to dismount him. But Edward struck his spurs into his horse, so that the beast rushed rapidly forward, and the Count, dragged from his own charger, was thrown heavily to the ground. Meanwhile the followers of both sides had fought with great eagerness and fury, until at last the trained skill of the English prevailed over the superior numbers of the Burgundians, and the Count of Châlon, foiled in his treacherous plan, was obliged to surrender his sword to a simple knight. Both sides suffered heavily, and the tournament became famous as the Little Battle of Châlon.

Edward now entered the domains of his cousin, Philip the Hardy, King of France. At the end of July he reached Paris, where he was entertained with great state. The cousins professed great affection for each other, but their love, as a shrewd French chronicler said, was like the love of cat and dog. There were important outstanding disputes. The cessions of lands in the south, promised by St. Louis in the Treaty of Paris in 1259 in return for Henry III.'s renunciation of all rights over Normandy, Anjou, and Poitou, had never been made. The French had not surrendered the royal rights in the bishoprics of Limoges, Cahors, and Périgueux (*i.e.* the Limousin, Quercy, and Périgord), which by the treaty were to have been yielded at once. Moreover, on the death in 1271 of Philip's uncle, Alphonse, Count of Poitiers and Toulouse and the precursor of direct French domination in the south, Philip had entered without scruple upon the possession of his vast inheritance, and laid hands upon Southern Saintonge, the Agenais, and Lower Quercy, which by the same Treaty of Paris were, on Alphonse's death without heirs, to fall to the English kings.

Edward was anxious to vindicate his claims to a share in the inheritance of Alphonse of Poitiers, but he could obtain no satisfaction from the astute clerks and knights who guided the policy of the dull well-meaning French king. All he could do was to perform the homage which as Duke of Aquitaine he owed to the King of France, in such ambiguous terms as to suggest that he still maintained his claims of right. "Lord King," said Edward to Philip, "I do you homage for all the lands which I ought to hold of you." With this reminder Edward quitted the French court, leaving his lawyers to continue the long-drawn negotiations with his suzerain.

Edward now went to Aquitaine, where his presence was urgently needed, and where he remained for more than a year. The duchy was still in that state of turbulence which, twenty years before, had proved too much even for the crafty policy and strong hand of Simon de Montfort. Moreover, the ministers of Philip of France were striving constantly to press forward their master's rights over the duchy, and the aggrieved vassals of the Duke of Guienne had grown well accustomed to appeal to the seneschal of Périgord, who watched over French interests in those regions. In 1273 there were two wars raging at the farthest extremities of Edward's French dominions. In the cold uplands of the north-eastern Aquitaine, the townsfolk of Limoges were carrying on a fierce struggle against their viscountess, and, mindful of the Treaty of Paris, called on Edward to protect them from her aggressions, which were the more formidable as they were backed up by the King of France. Edward at once espoused their cause. He sent his seneschal to Limoges to receive oaths of fealty from the burgesses. The men of Limoges took better heart as Edward's troops now joined their levies, and the joint forces inflicted several defeats on the viscountess. Unsuccessful in the field, the viscountess appealed to the court of King Philip for protection. In the autumn the French king announced his decision, which was dictated as much by his policy as by the law of the case. Edward was to renounce forthwith the fealty of the men of Limoges, and the viscountess was awarded full rights of jurisdiction over them. Edward faithfully accepted the situation, and abandoned his new subjects to the fury of their mistress. He construed his feudal duties very literally, and if he was punctilious in exacting his rights against his own vassals, it should not be forgotten that he was himself a pattern of feudal obedience to his own overlord the King of France. Flushed with his triumph, Philip now demanded that all Edward's Aquitanian vassals should take a direct oath of fealty to the King of France.

More formidable than the war of Limoges was the war of Béarn, whose Viscount Gaston, the leader of the feudal vassals of Edward, had contemptuously ignored a sentence of the ducal court, and held out defiantly in his Pyrenean strongholds. Edward led an army against his rebellious subject, and though he lost many men and horses from want of food, and from the difficulty of carrying on his campaign on the rough hillsides and deep-cut valleys of the Béarnese highlands, succeeded in reducing his enemy to the greatest extremities. Thereupon Gaston followed the example of the Viscountess of Limoges, and appealed to the French court. Philip then forbade Edward to pursue his attack on Gaston pending the hearing of the suit. Edward's ministers grew indignant, and urged their lord to disregard a command so injurious to his dignity. But the king's love of law triumphed over the impatience of his servants. He made a truce with Gaston, and having no further business in Aquitaine, started for England, travelling overland through France. On his way he negotiated at Montreuil-sur-Mer a treaty with the Count of Flanders, which settled an old-standing dispute that had for some time excluded English wool from the Flemish markets. On 2nd August 1274 he crossed over to Dover. Queen Eleanor had accompanied him in all his journeys.

The appeal of Gaston of Béarn dragged on for some time in the Parliament of Paris, the highest law-court of the King of France. The French lawyers wished well to the viscount's suit, but their strict regard for feudal propriety made it hard for them to overlook the violence, both of speech and act, which had marked Gaston's treatment of his immediate suzerain. Finally Philip advised Gaston to go to London, make his submission to Edward, and excuse himself for his misdeeds. Edward received his vassal's submission, but with characteristic lawyer-like subtlety he maintained that the submission was equivalent to a renunciation of Gaston's appeal to Paris, and that the sole point remaining was to determine the viscount's punishment. Philip saw that he was outwitted, but the situation became less strained since a personal reconciliation had followed Gaston's humiliation to Edward. The appeal was silently dropped, and in 1279 Gaston was formally reinstated by Edward in the fiefs which his contumacy had forfeited. The real triumph rested with the English king, and Gaston, for some years at least, kept the peace.

In 1279 the long-standing difficulties between Edward and Philip were brought to a satisfactory conclusion. In May Edward and Eleanor crossed over the Channel and took possession of the county of Ponthieu, which had just fallen to the queen as the heiress of her mother, Joan, the Dowager Queen of Castile and Leon and Countess of Ponthieu, who had just died. This county, whose capital was Abbeville, included a fertile region on the lower Somme. Philip of France now came to Amiens, where he was joined by Edward. On 23rd May the Treaty of Amiens, for which the diplomatists had long been working, was signed by the two kings. By it Philip ceded Agen and the Agenais outright, thus adding to Edward's lands the fair and fruitful plain of the middle Garonne. The French king also promised to submit Edward's claims over Quercy to a commission of inquiry, which eight years later assigned to Edward a large number of fiefs in the lower and richer parts of that region. Philip also renounced the oath of allegiance which he had demanded in 1275 of the Aquitanian vassals of Edward, a concession which he made with the more grace as very few of Edward's subjects had condescended to take an oath so contrary to French feudal custom. Moreover, he confirmed Eleanor in her newly won county of Ponthieu. In return for these great concessions, Edward solemnly abandoned all further claims on French territory. Thus the disputes which had been going on since the time when Philip Augustus had driven King John out of Normandy were finally brought to an end. Every important subject of contention between the two kings was removed. Edward had won great reputation both by the firmness and moderation with which he had pursued his ends. He had gained no small advantages in return for very shadowy renunciations, and had shown clearly to all Europe that the English king was not to be trifled with.

During the years of unfriendly negotiations between England and France, Edward had sought to strengthen himself on every side against a possible attack of his overlord. He had renewed friendly relations with his brother-in-law, Alfonso the Wise of Castile, though he had sought to protect the widowed queen Blanche of Navarre from the aggressions of her powerful neighbour. He had sought in 1273 to marry Blanche's daughter, the infant queen Joan, now nominal sovereign of Navarre and Champagne, to one of his sons, but though he failed in this, he succeeded in 1275 in marrying Blanche herself to his own brother, Edmund of Lancaster. Blanche was not allowed by the French to exercise her rights as guardian of her daughter in Navarre, but she still ruled over her husband's county of Champagne in her daughter's name, and Edmund was now associated with her as regent of one of the most important fiefs of the French crown, and, until his daughter-in-law attained her majority, he practically held the position of one of the great peers of France, and insured a powerful influence being exercised in his favour in all dealings with that country. Moreover, Edward had firm friends at Philip's court. Philip's mother, Margaret of Provence, was a sister of Edward's mother Eleanor. She was an enthusiast for the English alliance, and the strong influence which she possessed over her sluggish son, during the early years of his reign, may well be the chief reason that prevented the ever smouldering animosities of the two kings from breaking out into open war. But Margaret, like all her kindred, was a strong partisan of her family interests, and never turned her eyes away from those lands between the Alps and Rhone, which were now gradually slipping into French hands. She joined with her sister Eleanor in cordially hating Charles of Anjou, who had, with the hand of their youngest sister Beatrice, filched from the elder sisters the rich country of Provence, which he had used as a stepping-stone to his kingdom of Naples. Now Edward also hated the Angevin, who had supplanted his brother Edmund in his Italian kingdom, and had backed up the ruffianly Montforts, the murderers of his cousin Henry of Almaine. Urged on by his mother, who still exercised real influence over him, Edward willingly fell into any scheme which the fertile brain of his aunt could suggest against Charles of Anjou.

Margaret's plans all aimed at some sort of revival of the kingdom of Aries, that shadowy Middle Kingdom which had maintained a fitful existence as a borderland between France and Germany since the ninth century, but which had now been for nearly two centuries in abeyance, and split up into petty feudal states and subject only to the nerveless grip of a puppet Emperor, was slowly drifting towards incorporation with the French monarchy. She sought to raise up in the Arelate some rival power to Charles of Anjou. Her uncle, Philip of Savoy, was the natural supporter of a scheme which could not but strengthen his power at the expense of his Provençal rivals.

The King of the Romans, Rudolf of Hapsburg (he was seldom described as Emperor, as, like Richard of Cornwall, he was not crowned by the pope), also found one of his main interests in the revival of the Arelate. His election to the Empire in 1273 had ended the Great Interregnum, and had been largely due to the self-denying efforts of Gregory X. to restore to Europe its natural head. But the prestige of the Holy Roman Empire was almost dead. France, not Germany, was now the leading power, and the nominal successor of Augustus and Constantine owed nearly all his real power to the resources which he possessed in his hereditary dominions. Rudolf was but the lord of a scanty patrimony in Alsace and Swabia, and was unable to play any great part in Europe. But he was an energetic and active ruler, and did not limit his ambitions to Germany. Cut off from Italy by his convention with the papacy, he turned his attention to the Middle Kingdom, and found in Margaret of Provence and her nephew cordial and congenial allies. He now invested Margaret with Provence. It was but a formal act, but the form might well have been followed by very real results.

Edward now entered into the combination. In 1278 he signed a treaty by which his daughter, Joan of Acre, was betrothed to Hartmann, the

94

son of the King of the Romans. Among the lands assigned as Joan's dower were some of the districts which in the next generation became the seats of the infant Swiss confederacy. Rudolf despaired of getting his son chosen Emperor, but thought that the kingdom of Aries might be revived in his favour. With English and Savoyard support there seemed no small prospect of realising such a scheme, which, had it been carried out, might well have changed the course of later history by closing the lands between the Rhone valley and the Alps to French aggression. But a sudden change in the policy of the papacy dashed all these hopes to the ground. In 1280 a new pope, Nicolas III., faithful to the policy of Gregory X., succeeded in reconciling Rudolf and Charles, on the basis of establishing an equilibrium between them in the kingdom of Aries. To the deep disgust of Margaret and Edward, Rudolf abandoned the proposed English marriage, and accepted an alliance between his daughter and Charles's eldest son, by which the bride was to bring the Arelate as her wedding-portion to the Angevin heir. In 1282 Hartmann was drowned in the Rhine. However, it was not his death but the change of policy that preceded it that prevented Joan reigning over the Arelate.

The triumph of Charles over Margaret in the kingdom of Aries was the more bitter as it was attended by a still more signal victory over her at her son's court. About 1280 the specious and dexterous Angevin had insinuated himself so completely into the good graces of his nephew that Margaret's influence was practically destroyed. From 1280 to his death in 1285 Philip saw only with the eyes of his uncle, and abandoning St. Louis's policy of the gradual development of France, embarked in grandiose schemes of aggression in Spain and Italy, which simply served the Angevin interests. The results of this new policy of the French king were extremely important to Edward and England. The ink of the Treaty of Amiens was hardly dry when fresh difficulties arose with France on account of Edward's enemy obtaining the first place in Philip's councils.

The consequences were soon seen. Since 1276 France had been at war with Castile, and had laid violent hands on Navarre. Edward had laboured strenuously to bring about peace between Philip and Alfonso. In 1279, at Pope Nicolas's suggestion, a conference was fixed to meet at Bayonne, in which Edward was to act as mediator between his brother-in-law and his cousin. Then came the change of French policy which resulted from the triumph of Charles of Anjou. Edward's mediation was curtly rejected. Charles's son, the Prince of Salerno, was appointed mediator in his place, and even the King of Castile showed the utmost distrust of Edward. The English king was deeply annoyed. "You know," he wrote to Philip, "that I have wished to labour to bring about peace through my own efforts; but the King of Castile has discovered that I am too lazy and too sleepy to be entrusted with so delicate a task."

Edward's anger with Philip made him fall readily into the new intrigues by which Margaret of Provence sought to wreak her vengeance upon the Angevin. He sent his faithful seneschal of Gascony, the Savoyard John de Grailly, a man of great ability and experience, to assist his aunt in carrying out their plans. The widowed queen Eleanor threw herself actively into the scheme. Edmund of Lancaster and Champagne, disgusted that the French had taken Navarre out of his wife's hands, became an ardent partisan of Margaret. In the autumn of 1281 a crowd of feudal chieftains met at Macon in Burgundy, and pledged themselves to prosecute her claims over Provence by force of arms. In 1282 the parties to the League of Macon were to meet in arms at Lyons. Edward himself promised to send troops to the rendezvous. If he could not win the Arelate for his daughter, he might now hope to secure it for his kinsmen of the house of Savoy, to whom he was now, as ever, most warmly attached, but for whom, since the terrible experience of the Barons' Wars, he could do hardly anything on English soil. But the great plans of the confederates of Macon were never destined to be realised. The statesmen of the thirteenth century could form great plans of international intervention, but they seldom had force sufficient at their command to realise them. A motley league of feudal seigneurs could do but little against the Kings of France and Naples. Edmund of Champagne was too weak, Edward himself was too distant to be of much real help to them. Philip III. laboured vigorously to reconcile his uncle and mother. Margaret, despairing of the "way of warfare," was forced to leave her cause in the hands of her son's lawyers, who finally awarded her a money compensation for her abandoned rights over Provence. Edward's conduct all through was both honourable and able, and increased materially his position in the eyes of Europe. France, however, remained the real victor, and in 1284 the marriage of the heiress of Navarre and Champagne, Count Edmund's stepdaughter, to

97

Philip the Fair, the son and heir of Philip III., destroyed the last hopes of establishing a new English principality in France. Edmund's tenure of the regency of Champagne was thus abruptly brought to an end. As soon as his wife's daughter had entered into her twelfth year, its custody passed over to her youthful husband, the future King of France. Except in name, Champagne now lost its independence. It was soon destined to swell the domains of the French crown.

Renewed troubles now beset Edward in Aquitaine, which was still governed by the seneschal Grailly. But these sink into insignificance as compared with the great revolution which followed the Sicilian Vespers in 1282. The dominion of Charles of Anjou was thrown off with energy by the Sicilians, who called upon Peter, King of Aragon, to be their king. Charles, who maintained himself in Naples, now united with the pope in urging his nephew, Philip III., to join in a holy war against the Aragonese, who thus presumed to trespass on the lands granted to the Angevin by the Holy See. Edward carefully kept aloof from the quarrel. When a foolish proposal was made that the dispute of Charles and Peter should be fought out in a tournament at Bordeaux, he refused to take any part in so fantastic a business. "Know," he wrote to Charles, "that to gain two kingdoms such as Sicily and Aragon I would not be the umpire of such a battle; but I will strive manfully to bring about peace and concord between you." His earnest mediation produced no result. In 1285 Philip III. led a so-called Crusade into Aragon, but his army was discomfited, and he himself perished beyond the Pyrenees. His death marks not merely the end of a reign, but the end of an epoch. Within a few months Charles of Anjou, Peter of Aragon, and Pope Martin IV., the furious French partisan, were also in their graves. The new French king, Philip the Fair, at once withdrew from the Crusade. The new King of Aragon, Alfonso III., left to his younger brother James the dangerous and precarious throne of Sicily. The new King of Naples, Charles II. of Salerno, was a prisoner of his Aragonese rival. No party had force or energy to accomplish anything great, and all now longed for peace, and turned to the strong and impartial King of England as the one monarch in Christendom who was both able and willing to mediate between their conflicting claims.

Edward now saw a chance of realising his dearest ambitions. In 1286 he quitted England, and did not return until 1289. At Amiens he met the new King of France, Philip IV., who accompanied him to Paris, where he performed the homage due to his overlord for Guienne, and obtained a final settlement of his claims on Lower Quercy. Thence he travelled to Bordeaux, which became his headquarters for nearly three years. He at once busied himself in procuring peace between the French and Aragonese, sparing neither expense nor trouble to reconcile the fierce antagonists. At Christmas time he presided over a grand conference of envoys at Bordeaux. In the summer of 1287 he held a personal interview with Alfonso III., the new King of Aragon, at Oloron in Beam, where he succeeded in persuading Alfonso to agree to release the imprisoned King of Naples in return for a large ransom and a recognition of Alfonso's brother James as King of Sicily. Confident that peace was once more established in Europe, Edward again took the cross at Bordeaux, and busied himself with preparations for a new Crusade. But the pope repudiated the treaty, whereupon Edward set himself to work once more on his peaceful mission. In 1288 Edward concluded a second treaty, which resulted in Charles's release, Edward himself finding nearly all the money for his ransom. But no sooner was the King of Naples a free man than Pope Nicolas IV. released him from his oaths, and the war was renewed, though now limited to Italy. Edward warmly denounced Nicolas for stirring up warfare among Christian kings at the very moment when the Christian cause was at its last gasp in Syria. He sent an envoy to Italy, who procured a truce between the Kings of Naples and Sicily. Despite the furious partisanship of the popes and the greed and perfidy of the temporal princes, Edward had brought about his great work, the pacification of Europe. The successful mediator of the great peace now stood in the very foremost rank of European sovereigns. But all his hopes for a Crusade were doomed to disappointment. Urgent business called him back to England, and the pressure of the Scottish succession question and of constitutional difficulties at home diverted his mind from the affairs of the Continent.

The three years' sojourn of Edward in Aquitaine was an epoch-making period in the history of Gascony. Whatever leisure the great mediation allowed, Edward devoted to putting the affairs of his French dominions on a sound and satisfactory basis. He crushed a formidable conspiracy at Bordeaux, which sought with French help to undermine his power, and dealt out stern and rigorous justice to the traitors. Yet he did his best to promote the commerce of Aquitanian capital, and posed as the benefactor of all the cities of his duchy, seeking in them his best support against the turbulent feudal nobility. A characteristic part of his policy was the setting up of a class of new towns, called bastides, which were at once centres of expanding commerce, bulwarks of the English power, and refuges for the country-folk in times of war and trouble. Many of the most flourishing cities of Aquitaine look up to Edward as their founder. Some, such as Sauveterre, the safe land, suggest in their names the object of their establishment. Among all the bastides of Edward's foundation, Libourne, which took its name from the rising Tuscan port of Leghorn [Livorno], is perhaps the most important. Situated at the confluence of the Dordogne and the Isle, at the highest point where the wine -ships that traded with England could sail up from the sea, Libourne was admirably situated for trade, and no less well placed as an outpost of the military defence of Guienne against French aggression, and as a refuge in time of war for the neighbouring country-folk. It grew so rapidly that at one time it bade fair to be a rival to Bordeaux itself. It soon reduced to insignificance its older neighbours, like Fronsac, hidden away under the slopes of its vine -clad hill, and the more famous Saint Emilion, where a great military station had gradually grown up on the slopes of the strange amphitheatre, round which clustered the dense mass of houses that had gathered round the rock-hewn church of the hermit saint. Its plan, simple and regular as that of an American city, was that of all the class of bastides. Its eight main streets, as straight if not as broad as those of its American antitypes, radiated from a central square, wherein the public buildings were situated. Ample charters of liberties attracted a numerous population within its strong walls. But the modern Libourne contains but little that reminds one of the age of Edward. Its steady and long-continued prosperity has allowed but few memorials of the remote past to be seen in its busy streets. It is in some of the remoter and less prosperous of Edward's foundations that the characteristic features of the bastide type can best be studied. Little towns such as Beaumont and Montpazier, placed on the extreme north-east frontier of Edward's dominions, in the rolling hill country between the Dordogne and the Lot, and still far removed from railroads or great highways, preserve to this day in their quaint arcaded central square, straight-cut narrow lanes, fortified churches, and picturesque houses, walls, and gateways, an appearance not very dissimilar to that which they must have possessed when they were built, all at one time, at the bidding of their English duke. Yet even in his policy of founding towns in Aquitaine, Edward struck at no original line of his own. He was neither the first nor the only founder of bastides. Alphonse of Poitiers built the great bastide of Villefranche-de-Rouergue; St. Louis himself created one of the most important of bastides in the New Town of Carcassonne, still dominated by the wonderful fortress of the "Cite," crowning the steep hill beyond the Aude, whose walls, first set up by West Gothic kings and Languedocian counts, and restored to almost their present shape by St. Louis, still remain as the perfect type of a mediaeval stronghold. Every little prince and bishop followed the example of the greatest lords of the

102

south, and Edward was only one of a crowd of imitators. Yet he carried out his work of imitation with such energy and persistence that nowhere was the bastide type of town more thoroughly established than in his Aquitanian inheritance, and nowhere did the "new towns" have more important and lasting influence over the land which they both dominated and protected.

Edward busied himself with improving the administrative system of Gascony, and in attracting the Gascon gentlemen to the service of their dukes, both at home and in England. His seneschal John de Grailly gave him efficient assistance. He was one of the many Savoyards who had sought promotion in the lands ruled by Eleanor of Provence. Abandoning his home, now called Grilly, a few miles north of Geneva, he became by Edward's favour one of the territorial magnates of Aquitaine, and the founder of a house whose descendants three centuries later mounted the French throne. His elevation shows not only Edward's constant regard for his mother's people, but some sort of design of setting up new families unconnected with the region, and owing every thing to the king, as a counterpoise to the old feudal aristocracy. By such wise measures Edward laid the foundation of that close union of the duchy and kingdom which lasted through the storms and troubles of a century and a half. He could not change the conditions of his rule there, but he organised, and simplified the chaotic constitution of a feudal state. Nowhere can his claims to statecraft be better demonstrated than in his government of Aquitaine.

We have dwelt at perhaps disproportionate length on Edward's early continental policy. But no side of his career throws greater light on his statesmanship, and no side of it is less generally known in England. It has become the fashion to say that Edward's great merit was that he gave up all thoughts of the unprofitable Aquitanian heritage, and threw his whole energies into purely British questions. That Edward was above all things an English king, no one will deny. That the most important results of his work were seen in the organisation of English institutions and in the attempted extension of English rule over the rest of the British Islands is equally plain. But it is a very false and one-sided view that ignores his constant and vivid interest in his Aquitanian inheritance, and that puts aside as of no account his watchful care of English interests in Europe, and his constant efforts, in cases where direct English interests were very little involved, to uphold some sort of European balance, while strenuously striving to preserve or restore the peace of Europe. Edward's European policy was pre-eminently a policy of peace and mediation, but it is not to be ignored because his reign was marked by no great continental wars of his own seeking, and because it requires some effort to unravel the tangled threads of diplomatic negotiations through which Edward made his influence felt all over Europe. Not the least striking side of his policy of mediation is its amazing modernness. Yet Edward was above all others a man of the Middle Ages, though mediaeval aspirations after a Crusade jostle strangely with his modern conceptions of a political balance and a policy of interests.

But the truth is, that too much has been made of the contrast between mediaeval and modern; or, if we like it better, we may say that there was already a modern side in the policy of the great national kings who in the thirteenth century had begun to replace feudalism. There was a European political system before the days of Francis I. and Charles V., and there was need for a Wolsey in the thirteenth almost as much as in the sixteenth century. Thirteenth-century statesmen were not, as we are commonly told, altogether absorbed in home problems, and too feeble or too much wedded to routine and tradition to look abroad and take a comprehensive view of the European situation. They were as well able to plan the partition of a neighbouring state, or the degradation of a rival, as their descendants of modern times. What makes the real difference between them is, that they had not sufficient material resources at their command to carry out with any effect the bold combinations which they had plotted. Edward's favourite projects partake of this characteristic ineffectiveness, but, unlike Charles of Anjou or Philip the Fair, he limited himself for the most part to what was immediately practicable and immediately necessary. His wider schemes, such as those for the revival of the Arelate, show mediaeval statecraft in its feeblest and most impotent shape. But, when all deductions are made, Edward remains one of the greatest of English kings even in his foreign relations. He won for England a sure and foremost place in the councils of Europe. His honesty of purpose and his ability of conception have won the warmest praises both from his own contemporaries abroad and from those modern foreign writers to whose

105

works we must, to the disgrace of English scholarship, have recourse if we wish to learn how truly great was the great English king when all Europe welcomed him as the mediator of peace, when his friendship was sought by every power of Western Europe, and when he made the name of England respected and feared in Germany, in France, in Spain, and in Italy.

CHAPTER VI

THE CONQUEST AND SETTLEMENT OF THE PRINCIPALITY OF WALES
1274-1301

THE first serious difficulty that met King Edward in Britain was presented by the attitude of the Prince of Wales. Llywelyn ab Gruffydd had never cordially accepted the settlement of 1267. Flushed with the greatness of his triumph, he regarded the Treaty of Shrewsbury as but the starting-point for a fresh career of aggression. He never understood that the dexterous game, which he had played so well when England was divided, was the merest foolishness when the discord of king and barons was over, and when a strong king, ruling with the nation's good-will, stood in the place of the weak and irresolute Henry. Llywelyn was a man of vigorous character, high courage, and great dexterity and adroitness, but there was something of the barbarian about him, and he was slow to recognise new forces and tune his policy to altered conditions. He never realised that the Barons' Wars were over, and ever sought to pose with the English as the true successor of Earl Simon, hoping to thus win the hand of Eleanor, Montfort's only daughter, and to renew with the sons the close connection that had existed between him and the great Earl. But Edward I. was not Henry III., and the murderers of Viterbo were but poor substitutes for Earl Simon the Righteous. Moreover, Llywelyn was not content with the part which he had hitherto occupied as leader of the Welsh race. Inspired by the vain prophecies that credulity attributed to the wizard Merlin, and puffed up by the panegyrics of the bards and minstrels who revelled in his bounty, Llywelyn dreamed of a time when the Saxon should be expelled from the island of Britain and the ancient British race again rule over its old inheritance. He chafed therefore against the ties of vassalage that bound him to the English crown, and, profiting by the absence of Edward in the first two years of his reign, he resisted all the efforts of the regents to exact from him the customary homage to the new king. Nor did the return of Edward in 1274 mend matters. Llywelyn still excused himself, shuffled, and at last openly defied the royal mandates. The rough rule of Edward's ministers, the chronic disputes of the Welsh with the swarm of hostile Marchers, gave Llywelyn plenty of pretexts, and, in the eyes of his subjects at least, some sort of justification for his contemptuous disregard of feudal law. Edward was at last moved to profound anger. We have seen how he rigorously fulfilled the most irksome of his obligations as Duke of Gascony. He had no patience with the shifty Welshman, and sternly resolved to enforce his obligations by the sword. The Montforts established some connection with their old partisans in England, but Edward wisely checkmated their action by issuing a full pardon to the "Disinherited." The best of the baronial party were now on his side. Thomas of Cantilupe, Earl Simon's Chancellor, was Bishop of Hereford, and actively co-operating with Edward against Llywelyn. Nevertheless Amaury de Montfort, the most respectable of the sons of Simon, took ship with his sister Eleanor to

Wales that she might become the bride of Llywelyn. But some Bristol mariners captured the little squadron at sea. Edward put Amaury into prison and retained Eleanor in the queen's household. He paid no heed to Llywelyn's urgent appeals for their release. He was resolved that the Montforts should have no chance of reviving a party of popular opposition.

In 1276 there was war all along the Welsh border. In the early summer of 1277 the feudal levies mustered at Chester under the faithful Earl of Lincoln. Edward himself led the great expedition against Llywelyn. His early experience taught him the right method of warfare, and how best to win for himself allies among the Welsh. David, the brother of Llywelyn, fought under Edward's banner, along with the many Welsh chieftains who were jealous of Llywelyn's greatness. Broad roads were cut through the dense forests that then made dangerous the passage of the army from Chester to the Conway. A considerable fleet— mostly gathered from the Cinque Ports—sailed along the coast and kept the land forces well supplied with provisions and information. Llywelyn made scarcely a show of resistance, but retreated with all his men into the recesses of the great group of mountains which were in those days roughly known by the name of Snowdon.

Edward's plan was now to blockade his enemies in Snowdon. Every exit from the mountains was closed, while the fleet cut off all communications with Anglesey, whence alone Llywelyn could draw the supplies of corn necessary to keep his troops alive in the desolate regions of his retreat. Llywelyn held out a long time, but on the approach of winter he was starved into submission. Early in November he came down from the hills and accepted with what grace he could the hard terms imposed by Edward in the Treaty of Conway. By this convention the Welsh prince resigned all claims over the Four Cantreds of Perveddwlad and consented to hold Anglesey for his life only. He retained his other lands, along with the title of prince; but they were burdened with fines and a yearly rent for Anglesey, and he was forced to deliver up hostages for his good behaviour. Edward was, however, in no mood to exact these humiliating terms to the letter. He remitted at once the rent and the fine and sent back the hostages. Llywelyn now made his personal submission to Edward at Rhuddlan, and afterwards attended the Christmas court of his lord at Westminster, where he solemnly performed his long-delayed homage before the assembled magnates. The Welsh prince was now in high favour. Next year he held another interview with Edward at Worcester, where, in return for further submission, he was allowed to marry Eleanor Montfort. Edward himself attended the wedding ceremony. Llywelyn's brother David had received his reward in a rich estate in the vale of Clwyd.

The Treaty of Conway gave Edward an opportunity of renewing the plans of his early youth, and introducing the English shire system and laws into the ceded districts. The county court of Carmarthen and Cardigan, which had continued a sickly and precarious existence since its first establishment, was now revived, while the justice of Chester sought to subject the Four Cantreds to the jurisdiction of the Cheshire shiremoot. Meanwhile English traders and settlers came in the train of the English armies, and the castles that had first been established in the old days of Norman aggressions were now rebuilt and strengthened to keep down the subject lands. This policy excited the Welsh inhabitants of the ceded districts to the uttermost fury. They complained that Edward had shamefully broken the promise that he had made of ruling his new possessions according to their ancient customs and liberties. Edward answered that he would maintain the old Welsh laws so far as they were good ones, but that many of them were barbarous and directly at variance with the Ten Commandments. Such evil customs he could never observe, as he was bound by his coronation oath to uphold justice. This attitude was eminently characteristic. Edward's orderly and well-trained mind was disgusted at the barbarism of the old Welsh laws, and he honestly believed that he was doing his Welsh subjects the best service in his power in uprooting that venerable but primitive jurisprudence that allowed the murderer to atone for his crime by a money payment, and regarded wrecking as an unalienable right of the dwellers by the sea-shore. But Edward never understood the feelings of the Welsh at thus seeing their most cherished institutions trampled scornfully under the foot of an alien conqueror. His strong but somewhat narrow nature had few points of contact with the fiery, hot-headed enthusiasts with whom he had now to deal. He wished honestly enough that those Welsh customs should remain which were not against his conception of natural justice, but neither he nor his lawyers would put themselves in a sufficiently receptive attitude to understand them. At bottom Edward's real policy was to make

Welshmen Englishmen as soon as possible, and he was surprised that they resented his transparent sophisms, and murmured at reforms that he had only meant for their good. But now, as ever, Edward was badly served by his subordinates. The violence and brutality of his bailiffs and constables stood in damning contrast to his abstract talk about justice. His best friends among the Welsh fully shared in the national resentment to his policy. David himself was deeply hurt, and had quietly reconciled himself with his brother.

In the spring of 1282 the long smouldering hostility of the Four Cantreds to the English system burst out into open revolt. On the eve of Palm Sunday, David fell upon Rhuddlan Castle and took prisoner Roger Clifford, its guardian. Llywelyn hurried over the Conway to his assistance, and devastated the country to the very gates of Chester. A simultaneous rising broke out in the south, where the Welsh insurgents took possession of the new castle of Aberystwith, the key of Cardigan and Carmarthen. Edward was deeply enraged at the news of the new rebellion. He now resolved to make a great effort to finally crush the power of the Welsh prince. Archbishop Peckham of Canterbury put Llywelyn under the ban of the Church. Great armies were poured into both the northern and southern districts of the Principality. The strategy of 1277 was renewed. Llywelyn was again shut up in Snowdon, whither the Archbishop journeyed on a vain effort to induce him to submit. But Edward would accept no terms but unconditional surrender, though he gave a private assurance that Llywelyn should receive an estate of £1000 a year in England, with due provision for his

112

brother. But Llywelyn scorned such a degrading submission, and, mindful of his fate in 1277, escaped almost unattended from Snowdon before the winter snows again compelled him to surrender. He soon appeared in the Marches of the Upper Wye, hoping to raise a fresh revolt among the Welsh tenants of the Mortimers. On 11th December Llywelyn was slain in an obscure skirmish near Builth. David, who now called himself Prince of Wales, managed to hold out until the next summer, when his hiding-place amidst the bogs of Snowdon was discovered by the treachery of some of his own countrymen. With his capture the triumph of Edward was completed. A special Parliament was summoned to Shrewsbury to deal with the double-dyed traitor. On 3rd October 1283 David was hung, drawn, and quartered with the approval of the assembled estates.

The Principality was now conquered. Edward resolved that its future government should be put upon a solid basis. He remained in Wales almost continually until the work was done, living for the most part at Rhuddlan, and not finally quitting the country until the end of 1284. In the spring of 1284 he published at Rhuddlan the Statute of Wales, which contained the chief points of the new scheme. By it the Principality was declared annexed to the crown, and was constituted shire ground. The already existing shires of Cardigan and Carmarthen were set up in a more legal and complete manner. Though much smaller in size than the modern counties, they included the whole of the southern possessions of Llywelyn. They were put under a justice of West Wales who held his court at Carmarthen. In the same way the northern dominions of Llywelyn were divided into the three counties of Anglesey, Carnarvon, and Merioneth, the three old shires of Gwynedd. They were ruled over by the justice of Snowdon, who kept his state at Carnarvon, Sheriffs, county courts, coroners, and bailiffs were set up as in England, and a rough copy of English local government was thus introduced throughout the whole Principality. Edward's Welsh counties, as a modern writer has well said, bear to the English counties of this time some such relation as the Territory of the United States bears to the fully organised State. But it is to Edward's credit that he set up what form of local government he thought best in his new possession. And if at first the king's bailiffs and ministers had more power than in England, the administration of the Welsh shires fell almost from the first into native Welsh hands, and Edward made the new divisions more acceptable, by building them up out of the cantreds and commots which constituted the immemorial territorial divisions of the Cymry. A sixth Welsh county was also established by Edward in Flintshire, but this small region was for most purposes annexed to Edward's Palatinate of Cheshire, and Flintshire was for all practical purposes a mere dependency of the neighbouring earldom rather than an independent and autonomous shire. With the shire system came in a good many English laws, though Edward, made wise by experience, now took good care to uphold such Welsh customs as did not conflict with his sense of justice. But beyond these limits Edward's reforms did not go. His Welsh legislation left the Lords Marcher in the enjoyment of their disorderly feudal freedom, though the annexation of the Principality to the crown

114

largely diminished their political importance. The Marchers had helped Edward against Llywelyn, and he saw no good reason to disturb their vested rights, and probably feared to provoke the hostility of the many great English barons who would have certainly resented any infringement of their jurisdiction in their Welsh lordships. On the contrary, Edward erected new Lordships Marcher in those parts of the Four Cantreds which were not included in the new shire of Flint. The most important of these was the lordship of Denbigh, which Edward bestowed on his faithful follower the Earl of Lincoln. The result of all this was that the separation of Wales into Principality and Marches continued just as before until the reign of Henry VIII. It speaks well for the wisdom of Edward's legislation that it was as much from the Marches as from the Principality that Edward's subsequent Welsh troubles arose.

The subjection of the Principality was completed by the establishment of a strong line of castles and fortified towns. Edward now repeated in the Principality the policy already tried so successfully in Gascony. A row of "bastides" or "villes anglaises" were set up on the Menai and the Conway as on the Garonne and the Dordogne, to serve the same purposes of protection and defence, and to further in the same way the spread of commerce and civilisation. Archbishop Peckham advised Edward to make the Welsh live in towns and to send their children to school in England, for thus only, he declared, would the Welsh learn "civility." But Edward's object was not so much to attract the Welsh to live in his towns, as to settle in them little bands of

115

English soldiers, officials, and traders, who would prove, as in Ireland, the rallying points of an English interest. Though, luckily for both England and Wales, the townsfolk soon intermingled with the dwellers in the country, yet the history of Welsh towns is practically the history of English influence in Wales, and down to the days of Queen Elizabeth the separation so far remained that English and not Welsh was the ordinary spoken tongue of every market-town in Wales. But even more than the Welsh towns, the Welsh castles remain to this day a monument of Edward's power. The castle and walls of Conway, where fortress and town alike owed their existence to the Conquest; Carnarvon Castle, dominating the straits of Menai; and the rocky stronghold of Harlech, raised far above the waters of Cardigan Bay, are the best memorials of Edward's work in Wales. It has even been suggested that the well-known type of "concentric castle" to which these buildings belong, was first brought into the west by Edward, and based upon his observations in Syria of the mighty strongholds of the Latin Christians of Palestine. But Edward cannot claim this credit, and his boldest castles in Wales were but copies of the already existing Castle of Caerphilly, built a few years earlier by Earl Gilbert of Gloucester. Yet if Edward imitated the Marchers in building castles, the Marchers imitated Edward in setting up or granting charters to towns, so that the castle-building and town-foundation extended over Principality and Marches alike. The result was a great spread of civilisation, and Wales after 1284, though far from settled even according to the low standards of the Middle Ages, attained a far greater measure of peace and

116

prosperity after that the just though unsympathetic rule of Edward had succeeded the unending factions and the bloody wars of the native princes of Gwynedd.

Archbishop Peckham busied himself with the ecclesiastical reformation of Wales. Like Edward, he showed scanty respect for Welsh susceptibilities, but he did good work in rebuilding churches, raising the standard of church discipline, removing the married priests, and improving the education of the clergy. Moreover, he exhorted Edward to maintain fully the ancient liberties of the Welsh Church, and bitterly complained of the rash violence of Edward's officials, who "destroy and overturn every ecclesiastical usage that differs from the Anglican use to the no small peril of their souls." His highest desire was to see the Welsh better educated and accustomed to work for their living.

In August 1284 Edward celebrated his conquest by holding a "Round Table" tournament at Nevin in Carnarvonshire, where the most famous knights of England and the Continent fought amidst the wilds of Snowdon. Wonderful relics were opportunely discovered, including the body of Constantine the Great and the crown of King Arthur. The latter was presented to Edward. "Thus the glory of Wales," says the chronicler, "was transferred to the English."

Edward had no great difficulty with his new subjects during the rest of his reign. There were several revolts which threatened to become formidable, but the only one which really taxed his resources was that which Madog ab Llywelyn and his associates raised in 1294; and this owes its importance to Edward's other embarrassments at the time.

During Edward's long sojourn in Wales two of his children were born. One of these, Edward, soon became by his brother Alfonso's death his father's heir. His Welsh birth had already endeared him to Edward's new subjects, and he had a Welsh nurse and Welsh attendants to keep up his interest in the land of his birth. The stories that Edward presented him on his birth to the Welsh as their future prince have no more authority than the local tradition which points out as his birthplace a room in Carnarvon Castle, which is manifestly of later date. At last, in 1301, Edward created Edward Prince of Wales, thus keeping the Principality separate from the Crown, though retaining it in the hands of the royal family, and using it, as in his own father's time, as a means of training the heir in the work of government. It was a wise measure. Edward of Carnarvon was always a great favourite with the Welsh, who succoured him in his severest troubles, and celebrated his mournful fate in dirges written in their native tongue.

Edward I.'s whole Welsh policy brings out clearly his characteristic strength and weakness; but despite his narrowness and want of sympathy, his stern love of justice and equal laws made his policy in the long run a success, especially against a power whose open resistance he could crush with an overwhelming strength. He is generally described as the conqueror of Wales. More accurately he was the conqueror of the Principality. Yet he never sought to annex the Principality to England, although he incorporated it with the English crown. The Principality, like the Palatine county of Chester, or the still abiding liberties of the Lords Marcher, was still a land standing by itself. Save on two

118

occasions under Edward II., no members of Parliament were summoned to represent the Principality at the king's court. The king's writ and the king's English judges had no jurisdiction, and the whole machinery of administration remained separate and distinct. It was reserved for Henry VIII. to make England and Wales a single political unity.

CHAPTER VII

EDWARD'S LEGISLATION
1275-1290

THE thirteenth century was above all things the age of the lawyer and the legislator. The revived study of Roman law had been one of the greatest results of the intellectual renaissance of the twelfth century. The enormous growth of the universities in the early part of the thirteenth century was in no small measure due to the zeal, ardour, and success of their legal faculties. From Bologna there flowed all over Europe a great impulse towards the systematic and scientific study of the Civil Law of Rome. Side by side with the law of the civilians stood the rival legislative system of the canonists. The law of the Church rivalled the law of the State; the jurisprudence of the popes stood side by side with the jurisprudence of the emperors. Moreover, the northern lawyers were inspired by their emulation of the civilians and canonists to look at the rude chaos of feudal custom with more critical eyes. They sought to give it more system and method, to elicit its leading principles, and to co-ordinate its clashing rules into a harmonious body of doctrine worthy to be put side by side with the more pretentious edifices of the Civil and Canon Law. In this spirit Henry de Bracton wrote the first systematic exposition of English law in the reign of Henry III. The judges and lawyers of the reign of Edward sought to put the principles of Bracton into practice. Edward himself strove with no small success to carry on the same great work by new legislation. He had for his chief guide and adviser the chancellor Robert Burnell. A series of great judges like Hengham and Britton supplied him with practical knowledge. A great Italian jurist, Francesco Accursi, son of the more famous Glossator of Bologna, gave him the technical skill and the grasp of legal principle which were the great marks of the trained civilian; but the times were but little favourable to the acceptance in free England of the Roman law. The most popular law book of the reign—which later generations have ascribed to Chief Justice Britton—marks in this respect a going back as compared with Bracton. It is Bracton in substance, but Bracton rearranged, purged of his speculative aspect, and done into French that it might be more generally understood. It is very significant that the whole book is put into the mouth of King Edward himself, as if the whole law issued directly as the king's command. This alone shows that Edward was not regarded by his age as a merely passive instrument in the hands of his advisers. If he had not the originality to strike out new paths, he had at least the practical wisdom which absorbs and appropriates what is best in the common thoughts and actions of his age. Edward had an unerring eye for details, and great skill in ordering, arranging, and working out a legal principle to its utmost consequences. Since Henry II. had first systematised and arranged the legal system which grew out of the Norman Conquest, there had been a century of rapid development, fruitful in great and original ideas, but throwing out its results without order or method, and with little care for clearness or consistency. English law had grown like a great wood where the trees stand so close together that none attain their proper proportions, and where a rich tangle of underwood blocks up all paths and access. It was the work of Edward and his ministers to prune away this too luxuriant growth. Their work was a task of ordering, of methodising, of arranging. Edward's age was, as Bishop Stubbs tells us, a period of definition. His aim was to group together and codify, in such informal ways as the spirit of his age and country allowed, the legal system which had grown up in disorderly abundance in the previous generations. His well-known title of the "English Justinian" is not so absurd as it appears at first sight. He did not merely resemble Justinian in being a great legislator. Like the famous codifier of the Roman law, Edward stood at the end of a long period of legal development, and sought to arrange and systematise what had gone before him. Some of his great laws are almost in form attempts at the systematic codification of various branches of feudal custom. The whole of his legislation is permeated by a spirit which is at bottom essentially the same as the impulse which makes for codification. We shall therefore seek in vain for anything very new or revolutionary in Edward's legislation. We shall find a minute adaptation of means to ends, a spirit of definition and classification rather than any great originality or insight. But Edward did just what was most wanted at the time, and his work became all the more important and lasting because of its narrow adaptation to the needs and circumstances of his age. His work as a legislator puts him on a level with the greatest of the famous series of law -giving monarchs who adorned the thirteenth century. Neither St. Louis, nor Philip the Fair, nor Alfonso the Wise, nor even the Emperor Frederick II., attained a higher position as a legislator.

Edward was greedy for power, and a constant object of his legislation was the exaltation of the royal prerogative. But he nearly always took a broad and comprehensive view of his authority, and thoroughly grasped the truth that the best interests of king and kingdom were identical. He wished to rule the state, but was willing to take his subjects into partnership with him, if they in return recognised his royal rights. In the same spirit he ungrudgingly recognised the rights and immunities of the various orders of the State. St. Louis himself was not more careful than Edward in acknowledging the franchises of the baron, the clerk, or the townsmen, as they were understood by the general opinion of the age. But Edward, like St. Louis, was very careful to permit of no extension of feudal authority, and happier than his French uncle, was in a better position for enforcing the supremacy of the sovereign over all persons and in all causes. Just as he refused to be bound by the bad Welsh laws which went against his sense of justice, so he never brought himself to recognise any evil custom that trenched upon the inalienable and sovereign supremacy of the English crown. He would co-operate with the baronage in enforcing the feudal rights of the lords, but he never admitted that the feudal tenure of land gave the vassal any political rights that enabled him to set up a little state within the state. Thoroughly feudal as was Edward's conception of law and society, he laboured successfully in removing the last traces of the political effects of the doctrines of feudal tenancy. He narrowly circumscribed every old right; he refused to recognise any new ones. The same spirit marks his ecclesiastical legislation, for with Edward all his policy was a part of a concerted whole, in which there was very little that was irregular or capricious. A brief survey of the chief monuments of the secular legislation of his reign will show us the principles upon which Edward acted as a lawgiver. The details of his laws can only be profitably studied by the legal antiquary; but the broad principles on which they were based profoundly affected not only his own times but the whole subsequent course of English judicial history.

Edward's real reign begins with his arrival in England in August 1274. This event put an end to the peaceful government of the regency which had acted in his name since his father's death. Bold legislation now succeeds the monotony of administrative routine.

In 1275 Edward met his first general Parliament, and published as the result of their joint labours the Statute of Westminster the First. None of Edward's legislative acts better illustrate the position of the English Justinian. The whole ground of the law is covered in the long and comprehensive statute, which is almost a little code by itself. Next year saw the Statute *de Bigamis* and the Statute of Rageman, which instituted a special inquiry into cases of trespass. Far more important was the Statute of Gloucester of 1278, which was an attempt to strictly define and regulate the special franchises of the feudal barons. Nothing was more vexing to the orderly mind of Edward than the way in which the great immunities of the feudal lords broke up the regularity and uniformity of the administration of justice. He regarded the feudal jurisdictions as dangerous to the authority of the crown and as obstacles to cheap, sure, and uniform justice among the people. One of his first acts had been to send out commissioners to examine into the character and extent of the baronial immunities. The two large folios of the Hundred Rolls contain the results of this inquiry, which in its turn suggested the methods adopted by the Statute of Gloucester. Under this law fresh royal commissions traversed the country, inquiring by what authority the lords exercised their exceptional powers. Many of these franchises were found to be based on no specific charter, and to have no better warranty than ancient custom. But the very insecurity of their titles increased the anger of the baronage at the king's attack upon their vested rights. The great lords found a spokesman in the Earl of Warenne, who, though the husband of one of Edward's Poitevin aunts, and a strenuous upholder of the royal cause at Lewes, had no mind to see the ancient privileges of his order diminished. When the king's lawyers came with their writ of *quo warranto*, the Earl refused to base his rights on papers and parchments. He bared a rusty sword and exclaimed, "Here is my warrant. My ancestors came with William the Bastard and won their lands with the sword. With my sword will I defend them against all usurpers." Such an attitude taught Edward to proceed more cautiously. He made no more such direct attacks upon the political privileges of feudalism. He sought by indirect methods to compass an end that could hardly be procured openly.

125

Every year was marked by its great law. In 1279 Edward issued the Statute of Mortmain, which, though aimed most directly against the growth of ecclesiastical power, was but a part of Edward's general policy, and stood in close relation to his feudal legislation. The king, as the ultimate lord of English soil, had certain interests that were opposed to those of his tenants, while his vassals, in their capacity of lords over their mesne tenants, had in their turn certain common interests with Edward as lords. Edward now sought to approach the points of common interest, and thus to carry the great barons with him in a course which, though immediately equally advantageous to all lords alike, could not but prove in the long run to help forward the interests of the crown. The Statute of Mortmain sought to protect the rights of all lords of land, who were not seldom exposed to loss of their chances of relief, wardship, marriage, forfeiture, or escheat, by the transference of land held under them from an individual holder, whose heirs might be minors, unmarried, traitors or non-existent, to a perpetual ecclesiastical corporation that never died, that had perpetual succession, that could not commit treason, or fall into any of those feudal positions which gave to a lord the excuse for a fine or a forfeiture. The statute prohibited for the future grants of land to corporations whose "dead hand" never relaxed its grasp. We shall see later how important this statute was as affecting the relations between Edward and the Church. It was no less important as the first step of the union of king and baronage to protect the interests of the feudal lords, which ultimately produced the Statute of *Quia Emptores*.

126

The Welsh war hardly relaxed the legislative activity of Edward. Amidst the trials and troubles of the settlement of Wales, Edward found time to issue in 1283 the Statute of Acton Burnell, which gave merchants an easier way of recovering their debts, and in 1284 the Statute of Rhuddlan, which regulated the royal exchequer. But the return of Edward to England was marked by greater and more sweeping measures. The year 1285 saw the passage of two of the most important laws of the reign—the Statute of Westminster the Second and the Statute of Winchester.

The Statute of Westminster the Second has in its comprehensive character and wide survey of the whole field of legislative action no inconsiderable resemblance to the Statute of Westminster the First. It re-enacted and amended many of the greatest laws of the reign. It revived old laws, cleared up difficulties, proposed important amendments. But important as many of its clauses were, they sink into insignificance as compared with the famous first article, *De Donis Conditionalibus*, which had a most momentous bearing on the whole future land law of England. There had long been a custom of lords making a grant of land to a vassal or tenant under some condition. For example, a man might grant a piece of land to another to be held by him "and the heirs of his body." This was a "conditional gift," but it conveyed a full estate in fee simple to the recipient, except in so far as the succession after his death was limited by the words of the grant. But if the condition were fulfilled, the estate became in every respect like any other estate, like an estate in fee simple, which was at the complete disposal of the tenant for the time being. The grantee of an estate under condition who had a son born to him could if he liked sell the estate to somebody else. Also if he committed treason his "conditional estate" was liable to forfeiture. Such a state of things was, however, directly contrary to the interest of the capital lords. It was their obvious interest to limit the scope of the grant as far as possible, so that the chances of the estate reverting to their hands might be increased. Here the interests of Edward as the ultimate capital lord of the realm were exactly the same as those of the capital lord of every manor. The result was the Statute *de Bonis*, which provided that the rights of the heir of a conditional estate were not to be barred by the alienation of that estate by its previous tenant. The effect of this law was to create a new species of heritable estates, which were more limited in their scope than an estate in fee simple. They were called estates tail, because they were something "cut off" (*taillé*) from the fee. A further result was that estates of this description were tied up much more strictly than other estates. The tenant was but a tenant for life, and had no power of alienating or disposing of them in perpetuity. In a later age the action of the judges broke down the severity of the rule, but not before the habit had grown up of regarding entail as the rule and alienation as the exception. One characteristic feature of the English landed system was thus established. There were a large number of estates so strictly tied up that the actual tenant of them had but very limited power over them. It was thought a good thing to keep the property of a family as strictly as was possible within the grasp of the family circle. But many evils finally resulted from the practice, evils that the reforming legislation of our own day has hardly swept away. The unhappy coincidence of interest between Edward and his barons brought more harm to the land than the temporary confusions that would have resulted from the conflicts of the king and his lords.

The thirtieth article of the Statute of Westminster of 1285 worked a revolution in the English judicial system by instituting the justices of *nisi prius*, who were to traverse the country three times a year with a comprehensive commission that empowered them to hear nearly all sorts of civil suits. Fifteen years later a further act empowered the same justices to transact criminal business by acting as justices of gaol delivery, and proved a precedent for the further acts of Edward's grandson which concentrated on the itinerant justices all the various powers of the modern justices of assize. The result was a great simplification and economy of judicial force, a great saving to the crown, and a still greater relief to the people. Since the days of Henry II. it had been the custom to send round to the shires a constant swarm of royal justices, each with a very restricted commission. The counties were forced to entertain them, and they took good care that each visit should enrich the royal exchequer by a long series of fines and forfeitures. The result was that while the nation was burdened with their exactions, justice was often delayed for years, because it might so happen that the particular sort of court which was in request was only held at far distant periods. In consolidating and amalgamating the various judicial commissions, Edward added nothing fresh to the legal system of the country. Even in Bracton's time some justices were empowered to hear all sorts of pleas. But Edward made the rule of what had previously been the exception. Moreover, Edward by another act divided the country into definite circuits, and without any special legislation, his care for efficiency and zeal for definition led to the final and complete separation from each other of the three courts of common law—the King's Bench, Court of Common Pleas, and Court of Exchequer, with separate staffs of judges, each presided over by a special chief judge, and with special spheres of activity that were not yet evaded by the subtlety and pertinacity of a later generation of lawyers. Edward's reign also marks the establishment on a firm basis of the equitable jurisdiction of the chancellor. Burnell was thus both a chief minister and a great judge, and under him the chancellor bade fair to become a successor to the Norman and Angevin justiciar, a sort of prime minister.

The Statute of Winchester stands in strange contrast to the Statute of Westminster. While the latter is of the utmost importance in its bearing on later times, the former goes back to the earliest institutions of the land. It was an attempt to revive and reorganise the ancient popular jurisdiction of the local courts. It strove to give new life to the Hundred Court, the Fyrd, the Assize of Arms, and other ancient means of preserving peace and order by the action of the people themselves. It strove in particular to establish on the old lines a sufficient system of police. By the reinforcement of the military obligations which old English law had imposed on every freeman, it dealt another blow at the political importance of feudalism. It illustrates the conservative side of

Edward's policy, his care and respect for the primitive custom of the land. It also shows how he sought to define that custom and adapt it to new conditions. By it and other measures Edward passed in review the jurisdiction of the lower courts as well as he had dealt with the jurisdiction of the higher sources of justice. Nor did the petty courts of the manor escape his attention. The practice of recording the acts of the manorial jurisdiction in court-rolls seems to have first become universal during his reign. Thus Edward's fostering care gave firm consistency and definition to every branch of the judicial system. He was not only a legislator, but a judicial reformer of the first rank.

The years succeeding 1285 were not fertile in legislation. Between 1286 and 1289 Edward and Burnell were absent abroad, and the regent, Edmund of Cornwall, was not the man to plan great schemes of law-making. No sooner was Edward back in England than another great law was passed, almost the last practical and constructive piece of law-making in the reign. This was the Statute of Westminster the Third, better known from the first two words of the Latin text as the Statute *Quia Emptores*. This law, passed in 1290, stands side by side with the Statute *De Donis* in its importance for the history of the law of real property, while it marks, as regards the political aspects of feudalism, the secular counterpart of the Statute of Mortmain. Like *de Donis*, it provided for a case where the interests of the crown and the barons seemed at least to be identical. In 1285 king and lords sought to protect their interests by prohibiting alienation altogether on one large class of estates. In 1290 they strove to regulate the manner of alienating those

131

estates whose tenants were still free to dispose of them at will. Up to the passing of this act a man who held an estate in fee simple of a lord was free to aliene it either in whole or in part. If he gave up the estate altogether the new possessor simply stepped into his place, and stood for the future as he had stood in the past as regarded his relations with his overlord. But if a tenant of a lord wished to get rid of part of his estate, he could only do so by making the alienee his subtenant. He had, in short, to add a new link to the long chain of feudal dependence. The new purchaser was in consequence the under-tenant of the alienor, and stood in no direct relation at all to the overlord of the grantor. The result was often prejudicial to the interests of the overlords. Their rights over the land were diminished. The failure of the new owner's line would not give the overlord but his subtenant the benefit of the escheat. In the same way he would not have the guardianship or the right of marriage. Moreover, it often happened that the grantor aliened so much of his land that the part remaining was not enough to adequately discharge the feudal duties of the fief, and the absence of direct relations between overlord and the subtenant in the second degree made it easy to avoid discharging the obligations altogether. Hence the need, from the lords' point of view, for new legislation. Hence the Statute *Quia Emptores*, which provided that, in a case where a part of an estate was aliened, the alienee was not in the future to become the subtenant of the alienor, but was to stand to the capital lord in exactly the same relation as the alienor. The result was to prohibit all further acts of subinfeudation, and so to stereotype all existing feudal relations.

132

Before long it was clear that a deadly blow had been given to the feudal principle itself. The constant creation of fresh links of feudal obligation was a necessary part of the vitality of the system. The number of tenants-in-chief soon became very much greater, now that each sale of land by an existing holder-in-chief of the crown created a fresh tenant in capite, holding his land as directly of the crown as the alienor himself. It was soon found that feudal obligations became gradually relaxed, and finally sank out of sight altogether. In those cases where military service was the rent payable for an estate, some sort of feudal relation was kept up as long as the exigencies of local and border warfare still required from time to time the summons of the feudal levies. But in the numerous cases of socage tenure, where no rent was paid and no valuable service rendered, the empty obligation of fealty, which alone was left, soon fell into oblivion. The result was that it became a matter of no importance whether a man was a tenant in chief or a mesne tenant. Long before the act of Charles II. got rid of the very forms of military tenure, the legislation of Edward had effected its purpose. Tenure had no longer any political bearing. Even in its legal aspects tenure was rapidly becoming a matter of archaeological rather than practical interest. It was a fitting conclusion to the great legislative work of Edward's reign. For the seventeen years that remained of the great king's life, there was other work to be done. The attempt on Scotland, the struggle with Philip the Fair, the constitutional conflict with his subjects, were more than sufficient to occupy Edward's attention. Moreover, he had now lost his old helpers.

The great generation of lawyers died gradually away, and left no successors worthy to occupy their place. Burnell himself died in 1292, and the ministers of Edward's declining years had no share in the great and comprehensive schemes of law-giving which have given its peculiar importance to his reign.

CHAPTER VIII

EDWARD AND THE THREE ESTATES—THE DEVELOPMENT OF THE PARLIAMENTARY SYSTEM

THE same principles which influenced Edward as a lawgiver stand out clearly in his relations to every class of his subjects. Long before Edward had entered on his political career, the centralised despotism which Henry II. had built up had been overthrown, and the ideal of a limited monarchy, controlled by a great national council, and reigning in accordance with the principles of the Great Charter, had become dimly perceptible to the minds of Englishmen. But the strong tendency was to rely almost exclusively upon the great barons to keep the crown in check. The Oxford Parliament had set up a baronial oligarchy, which proved almost as oppressive to the nation at large as it was derogatory to the dignity of the crown. But the clash of interests between the crown and the barons forced both alike to fall back upon a broader platform, and to take into partnership with them the lesser landholders and the merchants and traders of the towns. This was the policy of Earl Simon, and this had been Edward's own policy, even before Montfort had gathered together his famous Parliament of 1265. The fuller realisation of the ideal rested, however, with the able and ambitious Earl. But no part of the heritage of Simon was more valuable to Edward than his uncle's policy of trusting in the people at large. It was the greatest work of Edward's life to make a permanent and ordinary part of the machinery of English government, what in his father's time had been but the temporary expedient of a needy tax-gatherer or the last despairing effort of a revolutionary partisan. Edward I. is—so much as one man can be—the creator of the historical English constitution. It is true that the materials were ready to his hand. But before he came to the throne the parts of the constitution, though already roughly worked out, were ill-defined and ill-understood. Before his death the national council was no longer regarded as complete unless it contained a systematic representation of the three estates.

All over Europe the thirteenth century saw the establishment of a system of estates. The various classes of the community, which had a separate social status and a common political interest, became organised communities, and sent their representatives to swell the council of the nation. By Edward's time there had already grown up in England some rough anticipation of the three estates of later history. The clergy had, through their special spiritual character and their common organisation in Church councils, acquired a very definite status of their own. The baronage had become narrowed down by the strong tendency of the lesser tenants in chief to dissociate themselves from the great lords, and act with the mass of the lesser gentry in the shire courts. The policy of Montfort had already brought together the knights of the shires and the representatives of the towns in a single organised community. By dexterously combining the new system of estates with the old ideas of local representation, Edward erected the

136

estate of the commons as a necessary part of the machinery of the constitution. He is also in a very real sense the creator of the House of Lords. It was no fault of his if the clerical estate did not also take up its part side by side with the two more permanent elements in our later constitutional life.

In regard to this development of the system of estates, Edward's relations to the various classes of the community assumes a special importance. It will be necessary to speak later of his uneasy dealings with the clerical body; but the course of the development of our parliamentary institutions can perhaps be made clearer by a short account of Edward's early attitude towards the barons and the commons.

During the earlier part of Edward's reign the baronial opposition, which had so constantly kept his father in check, had almost no existence at all. The barons were perhaps a little suspicious of some of Edward's legislative tendencies, and we have seen how the opposition to the writs of *quo warranto* might easily have produced another organised effort at resistance. But Edward, by his careful regard for his barons' legal rights, gradually won their complete confidence. His policy of legal reformation, in those directions in which the king and the barons had a common interest, did much to strengthen his good relations with the great nobles.

So far as there was any baronial opposition to Edward at this period, its leader was Earl Gilbert of Gloucester. The Red Earl's extreme tenacity in upholding his own rights was constantly embroiling him with his neighbours. His love of strong-handed local feuds often involved him in private wars which were altogether hateful to Edward's orderly and law-loving mind. More than once his relations with the king were very strained. At one time he was suspected of sheltering Welsh fugitives in his Irish estates. He was on very bad terms with his wife, Alice of Angouleme, Edward's Poitevin cousin, whom he ultimately divorced. At last, in 1288, he headed the baronage in refusing to pay any subsidy until the king came back to England. But in 1290 his hostility was bought off by his marriage with Joan of Acre, Edward's daughter, though a year later he carried on open war against the Earl of Hereford for the possession of the Marcher lordship of Brecon. But for this contumacy both earls were fined and imprisoned; and Earl Gilbert's death in 1295, just before the reconstitution of a baronial opposition, prevented him from ever having again the opportunity of renewing the turbulent scenes of his youth. His attitude was typical. If Earl Gilbert could find so little to oppose in Edward's policy, the mass of the barons had still less to say against it. And it was in the years of this absence of opposition that Edward carried through the organisation of the historical House of Lords.

Edward's dealings with the commons are more complicated. There is little to show that he was often in opposition to the shire communities. On the contrary, the statesman, who in his youth had been the greatest upholder of the political claims of the knighthood, continued to find in the gentry of England his best and strongest support. It was otherwise with the towns, with whom Edward was constantly quarrelling. This was due largely to his constant financial embarrassment, and especially to his tendency to bargain with the foreign merchants, who, in return for increased facilities for carrying on their trade, made him large grants of money, and that the more willingly as what they conceded to the king came ultimately out of English pockets. But the memory of the Barons' War was not yet quite dead, and had a great deal to do with the exceptionally bad relations between Edward and London.

London was now ruled by a civic oligarchy, whose most conspicuous leader, Henry le Waleys, a wine merchant, and probably a Gascon by birth, was on many occasions Mayor of London and once Mayor of Bordeaux. The rule of this body seems to have been politically offensive to Edward, and not very successful in maintaining order. After many quarrels Edward took a decisive step in 1285. He ordered the mayor to appear before the treasurer, John Kirkby, who kept his court in the Tower. The mayor attended, but he declared that his summons was against the franchises of London, and that he appeared but as a simple citizen anxious to show respect to the king's representative, and not as an official. Thereupon Kirkby "took the mayoralty and liberties of the city into the king's hand, because the city was found to be without a mayor." A royal official, Ralph Sandwich, was made warden of the city, and from 1285 to 1298 the Londoners were deprived of their right of electing their chief magistrate, and forced to pay obedience to a royal nominee. In other respects their liberties were preserved, and, as at Bordeaux, Edward did his best to encourage their trade. Perhaps Edward's hostility to the Londoners accounts for the great efforts made by him to encourage the growth of other towns. He was, moreover, one of the few English statesmen who have definitely founded new towns in England, and he chose the sites for his new foundations so well that they have for the most part subsequently prospered. When Old Winchelsea was overwhelmed by the sea, Edward founded New Winchelsea, which, until the sea receded from its walls, remained one of the great ports of Southern Britain. He also established the town of Hull, which took from him its full name of the Kingstown-upon-Hull. These foundations show how the ideas which Edward had already realised in Gascony and Wales were extended to England. But despite his uneasy relations with certain towns, Edward was fortunate in the early part of his reign in meeting with so little opposition from the estate of the commons.

Edward's high-handed dealings with the English towns show how tenacious he was of his prerogative. It was with no intention of diminishing his power, but rather with the object of enlarging it, that Edward called the nation into some sort of partnership with him. The special clue to this aspect of his policy is his constant financial embarrassment. He found that he could get larger and more cheerful subsidies if he laid his financial condition before the representatives of his people. Apart from the special difficulties which Edward inherited, there were more general causes for his financial distress. We have seen already how the elaborate machinery of government set up by Henry II. was rapidly becoming obsolete. Now this partial breakdown of the Angevin system extended to its financial organisation, and the complex arrangements which made the sheriff the king's general tax-gatherer was already becoming worn out. Edward was therefore forced to seek new sources of revenue for himself. One such stream of income he found in the ancient tolls or duties levied upon merchandise of all sorts, both on its coming into and leaving the realm. The growing commerce which attended a more settled state of society and a better system of government made these duties or customs more important and valuable than they had been before. For the same reason the rude old way of levying the customs by taking a certain portion of all goods sent in or out of the realm for the king's use became irksome to the traders and unsatisfactory to the king. In 1275 accordingly Edward agreed, with the same Parliament that passed the Statute of Westminster the First, to accept a specified custom in money in lieu of his rights of prize over the staple commodities of English trade, conspicuous among which were wool and leather. Thus originated the *Ancient Custom or Great Custom*, which remained for the rest of the Middle Ages an important source of royal revenue. But the king's vague old rights still remained, except in the case of certain specified commodities, and in times of distress Edward could not resist laying violent hands upon a larger share of the merchants' goods than he had any customary or statutable right to possess. His violent and excessive *Maltoltes* provoked a storm of opposition in the great crisis of his reign which ended in 1297 with their formal abolition. But even after this Edward made a special bargain with the alien merchants trading to England, who in return for certain trading privileges granted him in 1303 a New Custom, which, after

141

much opposition, was at a later time accepted by the representatives of the nation. Meanwhile Edward had gradually organised and developed a better system of collecting the Customs revenue. But as he handed over its collection to companies of Italian merchants, much of it, no doubt, never reached his hands. Edward was still forced to seek for further supplies. He was therefore compelled, as his predecessors had been, to have recourse to the representatives of his people, and asked them for many direct parliamentary grants and subsidies. Hence the close connection between the financial and the parliamentary history of the reign.

Edward's early parliaments strike us as very chaotic and anomalous. One year the king assembled the knights of the shires, but next year he was contented with summoning the barons and bishops. And both the full representative parliaments and the old-fashioned baronial parliaments seem to have discharged exactly the same functions, and to have been looked upon as of equal authority and competence. In 1282 Edward fell back on an even more ancient expedient. He sent John Kirkby, his trusted financier, on a tour round the different shires and boroughs, and asked each community separately to help him to bear the cost of the war against Llywelyn. The answers being inadequate, the king summoned knights of the shire and borough representatives to meet side by side with the clergy in two assemblies, the one for the province of Canterbury and the other for that of York, thus modelling a secular parliament on an ecclesiastical council. The response of these anomalous bodies proved so far satisfactory to Edward that he never seems to have fallen back upon negotiations with the local courts. The result was a step in advance. Local and individual consent to taxation was superseded by national and general consent, and the old notion of a tax as a voluntary grant to the king was replaced by the more refined conception of it as a universal duty of citizenship. In strong contrast to the parliaments of 1282, Edward summoned in 1283 a parliament to Shrewsbury that contained nobles, knights, and burgesses, but no clergy. The composition of a parliament seemed still to depend upon the nature of the business to be laid before it. So late as 1290 a merely baronial parliament passed the important Statute *Quia Emptores*. The third estate was summoned, but its representatives only appeared after the act was passed. It was a question for the barons specially, and the commons had no need to concern themselves with it.

The period of experiment now rapidly passed away. Various as are the elements of Edward's early parliaments, yet we can still see the direction in which the current was steadily setting. People were getting so accustomed to the presence of the popular element that it had almost become the exception for it to be absent. Then came a period of crisis—a time of unsuccessful war abroad, of sedition at home, of rebellion in the newly-annexed districts, and of open war with the great power of the Church. Edward felt that he could only meet his difficulties if he got the support of the mass of the nation on his side. He also realised that it was only by national grants that he could permanently keep up sufficient forces to get the better of his enemies. He enunciated the great and pregnant maxim that what touches all should be approved by all. In 1293 and 1294 large representative parliaments laid great burdens upon the nation, but upon the practical condition that it was necessary to ask the clergy and the commons for their consent before any taxes could be constitutionally imposed upon them. In 1295 a further and final step was taken. Edward then assembled a parliament so full and complete that it rightly became looked upon as a Model Parliament for succeeding ages. To it came the earls and barons as a matter of course. But by their side gathered two knights chosen by the popular court of each shire, and two citizens or burgesses from every city or borough town, summoned like the county members by writs sent in the first instance to the sheriff of the shire. Moreover, the clergy was also fully represented. The archbishops, bishops, abbots, and other dignitaries down to the deans and archdeacons, were there in person; but each chapter also sent its proctor or representative, and the parochial clergy of each diocese sent in the same way two proctors. The result was a complete parliament of the three estates. From this year no other great council can be regarded as possessing supreme and exclusive power in matters of great weight. In the great parliaments in the later years of Edward's reign the precedent set by this famous assembly was carefully followed.

The parliament of 1295 suggests a comparison with the parliament of 1265, but its differences are as instructive as its similarities with the earlier and perhaps more famous assembly. Both were roughly based upon the same broad lines of general national representation; and it was the good fortune rather than the merit of Edward that the parliament of 1295 was a real gathering of the whole nation, and not, like that of 1265, a mere parliamentary assemblage of partisans of the dominant faction. By summoning the borough members by writs addressed to the sheriffs of the counties, Edward effected one important improvement in detail on the arrangement of Simon, who had sent the borough writs direct to the towns themselves. Edward's practice afterwards prevailed, and had the good result of teaching the townsfolk to look upon themselves as parts of the shire, and not as isolated communities cut off from the life of the nation at large. But the really important thing was that Edward, like Montfort, brought shire and borough representatives together in a single estate, and so taught the country gentry, the lesser landowners, who, in a time when direct participation in politics was impossible for a lower class, were the real constituencies of the shire members, to look upon their interests as more in common with the traders of lower social status than with the greater landlords with whom in most continental countries the lesser gentry were forced to associate their lot. The result strengthened the union of classes, prevented the growth of the abnormally numerous privileged nobility of most foreign countries, and broadened and deepened the main current of the national life. Moreover, in the summonses issued to the baronial class Edward strictly limited himself to a small and restricted number of magnates. No doubt the main lines on which the barons were summoned were marked out for Edward by long precedent, but it was left to the king and to no other to draw the exact line where he did. The "lesser barons" of the Angevin times—the smaller tenants in chief—no longer received a baronial summons, for Edward, faithful to his doctrine of the elimination of tenure from politics, forced them to throw in their lot with the mesne tenants in the shire courts, and be represented by the chosen men of the shire community at large. The special writs now issued to the few score of remaining barons were looked upon as practically involving the summons of their successors as well. Though life peers by no means disappeared altogether, the custom of hereditary peerage was also established by Edward's action. The lawyers have always held that the male heirs of those whose lawful ancestors received a summons to his model parliament can claim a right to a writ of summons. Even more than the House of Commons, the House of Lords thus largely owes its limited and hereditary character to the action of Edward and his advisers. The clerical estate did not, however, long retain its position in parliament. The separatist class feelings of the clergy, the irksome tie of papal obedience, and the extravagant immunities which mediaeval tradition allowed to the spiritual caste, were all unfavourable to their remaining on the same lines as the other estates. Moreover, the clergy had in their provincial councils or convocations assemblies whose constitution was essentially similar to that of the clerical estate in parliament, and whose composition was being fixed and defined by Archbishop Peckham, in the same way and at the same time as Edward himself was defining the composition of parliament. In after ages the clergy preferred to tax themselves in convocation, and kings, anxious to avoid difficulties, let them have their way. Meanwhile the bishops and abbots, who, like the earls and barons, were also magnates, sat side by side with the secular lords, with the result that the next century saw the establishment of the two houses of Lords and Commons, instead of the three separate gatherings of the three estates which might have been anticipated from Edward's action in 1295. But to trace this process would carry us far away from the biography of Edward. Enough has been said to show how important a part the great king played in the development of our parliamentary system.

At the same time Edward's neighbours, the kings of Western Europe, were engaged in the same task of building up a national kingship on the basis of a representative system of estates. The work of Edward has alone in any way survived. The wildest upholder of the claims of Edward to greatness would not ascribe to him the sole or the main merit of this superior permanence. The reasons for it are deeply seated in the whole of the previous and subsequent history of England. Yet we must not forget that our national pride in our own institutions has led us to exaggerate rather than minimise the differences between thirteenth -century England and her main continental neighbours. There is, in truth, hardly such deep gulf as has been commonly supposed between the England of Edward and the France of Philip the Fair; between Edward's parliament and the States-General which Philip called into being to resist the forces of Roman aggression. What differences there were certainly lay in favour of England, where a happier past had produced a broader and richer stream of continuity from remote ages, and where there existed institutions and traditions that made for nationality, and did not rest on the personal basis of a despot's goodwill. But some share at least of the credit of the superior success of the working of parliamentary institutions in England may not unjustly be set down to the credit of Edward. His skilful union of national and dynastic purpose, his selection of the best and most fruitful precedents, his strong good sense and business-like adaptation of means to ends, all united to further the growth of that national parliamentary constitution which, though its roots lay deep in the past, took under his auspices the shape and form which it retained with but little variation until the Revolution of 1688, and even, so far as externals went, until the Reform Bills of the present century, following the true spirit of Edward, recast the old institution to meet new and changed necessities.

CHAPTER IX

EDWARD AND THE CHURCH
1272-1294

THE relations of Edward to the Church shed a strong light on his policy and character. Edward was himself a man of sincere and ardent religious feeling. He was rigidly orthodox, and never so much as questioned the right of the Church to reign supreme in all matters of faith and practice. A crusader in his youth, he never, as we have seen, altogether relinquished his hope of joining in a great movement for the recovery of the Holy Sepulchre. He was an unwearied attendant at the offices of the Church. He was a founder of monasteries and an ardent pilgrim to holy places. To what he conceived to be lawful ecclesiastical authority he yielded an absolute and ungrudging obedience. Yet Edward's personal piety and unblemished orthodoxy did not prevent the greater part of his reign being occupied in a long and stern fight both with the papacy and with the leading representatives of the national Church. And it was inevitable that this should be so. The thirteenth century witnessed both the culmination of ecclesiastical pretensions and the first vigorous growth of that national power which was in the long run to subject the Church to itself. It was an age of strange contrasts. The successors of Pope Innocent III. indulged in dreams of universal domination such as would have appeared strange to a Gregory VII. or

149

an Alexander III. Their pretensions could not but trench upon the political sphere. The chronic difficulty of determining the relations of the king, as the representative of the nation and the secular arm, with the pope, as the recognised head of the Church universal, was never presented in a more perplexing and bewildering form than to Edward. And the difficulty of the situation was increased when we remember, what some moderns would fain forget or ignore, that to every Christian of the age of Edward the pope was the divinely appointed head of the Church, with large judicial and taxative powers over the whole of Christendom, and the main if not the sole source of ecclesiastical jurisdiction. Yet hard as was the question of determining the royal relations to the papacy, the difficulties of this side of the problem sink into insignificance as compared with the difficulty of determining the relations between the Crown and the national Church itself, where all through the Middle Ages the chronic conflict of Church and State was wont to assume its bitterest and most irreconcilable form. A strong king like Edward, who was resolved to be really supreme over the State, and who waged constant war against all forms of class privilege, could not but stand in an attitude of permanent hostility to the pretensions of the clerical caste to absolute immunity from the secular jurisdiction, and to the constant tendency of the ecclesiastical high-fliers to treat the State as a mere means for carrying out the will of Holy Church. Yet though there was a constant undercurrent of opposition between Edward on the one side, and the Roman Curia and the English hierarchy on the other, it is no small testimony to the tact and skill of the king that these

150

chronic difficulties came so seldom to the surface, and that the reign passed by without a new struggle on the lines of that of Henry I. with Anselm or Henry II. with Becket, and that even the fierce fight of Boniface VIII. with Philip the Fair awoke but a faint echo in England.

In treating of Edward's ecclesiastical policy we must distinguish between his dealings with the papacy and his dealings with the English Church. We must further remember that in the Middle Ages, even more than in our own time, the Church did not form a single corporation and hardly a single organisation. The Church included in its ranks every class of society, every variety of lawful opinion. It is unreasonable then to expect any unity of action from so great and many-sided a body. In the same way too much precision must not be given to the distinction between the English Church and the Church universal as represented by the papacy. In the thirteenth century no hard and fast line can be drawn between the two. The ecclesiastical problem was sometimes presented in a two-fold aspect, on other occasions in a single one. Moreover, the great religious revival, which had witnessed the establishment of the Mendicant Orders, had tended on the whole to bridge over the gulf between the Roman Curia and the National Church. Edward's difficulties were therefore for the most part presented to him in a complicated form.

Edward had been brought up to look upon the papacy as the undoubted superior of the English crown, both in Church and State. The humiliating submission of John to Innocent III., by which England had been formally constituted a papal fief, was still so recent in men's minds that it almost effaced the fading memory of the times when England was another world in matters ecclesiastical, and when the ties which bound England to the Roman see were scarcely more substantial than the ties which now bind Canada or Australia to the mother country. All through the Barons' Wars, Henry III. had made unsparing use of the friendship of the Roman Court, as a convenient weapon against his rebellious subjects. He obtained from two successive popes a release from his plighted oath to observe the Provisions of Oxford, and Edward himself had not scrupled to take advantage of the same papal dispensation. Yet all the thunders of the papacy had not detached a considerable section of the best of English Churchmen from the patriotic side. The good bishop, Walter of Cantilupe, had blessed Earl Simon's soldiers as they drew up to meet the royalist forces on the field of Lewes. The nameless scholar who wrote in the Song of Lewes the clearest statement of the principles and policy of the baronial party; the mass of the monastic chroniclers who describe with ardent partisanship the mighty deeds of Montfort for the good cause; the simple priests and laymen who worshipped the dead earl as a saint, were all alike careless or hardly conscious that their hero died under the ban of the Roman Church. Now Edward was at least as much the heir of Montfort as the inheritor of the policy of his father. His heart was at least as much stirred by the patriotism of the native English Churchman as by the thunders of a papal legate. He parted, unwillingly enough, yet none the less thoroughly, with the foreign bishops and clerks, who had come in the train of the foreign lords and ladies. It was his difficult task to

152

absorb and appropriate the national Church feeling which had stood so strongly on the side of Montfort. At the same time he could foresee an endless series of difficulties if he abandoned his father's friendship for the papacy. He realised very fully the utility of papal support in carrying out both his English and his general European policy. Moreover, Edward was fully conscious of the need of keeping up the traditions of the absolute supremacy of the Crown, which William the Conqueror and his sons had upheld and handed down as a binding tradition to later ages. Priests no less than laymen must submit themselves to the king, who was not less truly the Lord's Anointed than the bishop or the abbot. Like the lords of a feudal franchise, the clergy might continue to rule within their own sphere; but it was Edward's constant care to define that sphere as narrowly as circumstances allowed.

The first step to set aright the relations of Church and State was to secure for friends of the king the chief posts of the Church as they fell vacant. In the early period of his rule Edward was more lucky in his personal relations to the popes than to his archbishops. Just as Edward was starting for his Crusade, the death of his unworthy uncle, Boniface of Savoy, had ended the weak and nerveless tenure of the primacy of the English Church by one of the most hated of the queen's kinsmen. Edward, who always stood by his friends, made `a vigorous effort to secure the election of his favourite clerk, Robert Burnell, to the vacant archbishopric. Disgusted that his letters provoked no response, Edward hurriedly abandoned the preparations for his embarkation and hastened to Canterbury. The monks of the cathedral of Christ Church, in whom the canonical right of election was vested, were deliberating in the chapterhouse with locked doors. Edward violently burst open the fastenings and, almost beside himself with rage, vehemently urged the frightened monks to choose his friend as their archbishop. But not even the ravings of the king's son could force the clannish monks to elect a secular clerk. Edward withdrew in impotent anger, and started at once on his Crusade. The monks chose in due course one of their own number, but Gregory X. persuaded the candidate of the chapter to resign his claims. When Edward came back to England as king he found the pope's nominee, Robert Kilwardby, seated upon the throne of St. Augustine.

Kilwardby was a Dominican friar, and the first Mendicant vowed to absolute poverty who occupied a high place in the English Church. He was a learned theologian and a famous master of scholastic dialectics, an ardent churchman, a strong papalist, and an upright and honourable man. His appointment was probably due to the desire felt at Rome that the new archbishop should be a zealous upholder of the extremest ecclesiastical pretensions. But the excellent understanding that prevailed between Edward and the good pope Gregory X. prevented any possibility of conflict as long as Gregory lived. Succeeding popes found a further difficulty in pushing forward their claims, in the limited interests and senile inactivity of the Dominican archbishop. So thoroughly did Kilwardby disappoint the hopes which the papal Curia had formed of him, that in 1278 he was dexterously removed from his see by his translation to the cardinal-bishopric of Porto. In the thirteenth century the cardinalate had not yet become that merely honorary dignity which might be fitly borne by the primate of a remote transalpine province. The cardinals were still bound to residence at the papal court, and promotion to the purple involved therefore the abandonment of such distant preferment as the English primacy. Kilwardby accordingly gave up his archbishopric, and meekly accepting the covert censure implied in his formal promotion, took up his residence at the papal court, where he died soon afterwards.

Edward made a second effort to promote Burnell, now Chancellor and Bishop of Bath and Wells, to the archbishopric of Canterbury. This time the monks of Christ Church interposed no obstacle, but Pope Nicolas III., after appointing a special commission to inquire into Burnell's fitness, declared that circumstances had come to his ears which made it impossible for him to accept Edward's minister as archbishop. It was probably the scandalous looseness of the great chancellor's private life which gave a good reason to the pope for refusing to advance to so high a post a man so absolutely devoid of high clerical ideals and hierarchical pretensions. Two years later Nicolas would not even allow Burnell's translation to Winchester. Thus did his strong friendship for his minister and his desire to reward him adequately for his good service to the State expose Edward to two well-merited rebuffs from Rome, as well as to the scandalous imputation of desiring to make the great places of the Church mere rewards for political good service.

Nicolas III. now appointed an archbishop of his own mere motion. His choice fell on John Peckham, a Sussex man, a Franciscan friar, a famous doctor of theology and writer upon optics and mathematics, who at the time was a teacher at the university of the papal court. Peckham was not less distinguished for his learning than for the austerity of his life. He fasted seven Lents in every year, and performed all his journeys, however long, on foot, disdaining the paltry evasion of the rule forbidding friars to ride on horseback, which led Mendicants of less austere principles to travel on mules or asses. He was an active, bustling, fussy man, pompous in his talk and gesture, with little tact, but unbounded energy and zeal, devoted, as the best spirits of his order then were, to the highest doctrines of papal infallibility and hierarchical power, but transparently honest and absolutely devoid of self-seeking. He started for England conscious of a high mission to stamp out immorality, laxity, and pluralities, and to put an end to the rule of worldly bishops and careless kings over the Church of England.

Edward was high-minded enough to bear no malice, and received Friar John with a kindness that the new archbishop cordially and gladly recognised. But no personal motives could turn Peckham from the strict path of duty. As soon as he got to England he summoned a Church council to Reading. This assembly passed at the archbishop's instigation a series of thorough-going canons against pluralities, an act which excited the alarm of the benefice-hunting clerks of the king's household. It also ordered the clergy to hang up in every great church a copy of Magna Carta, and to denounce periodically all offenders against

156

the Charter as *ipso facto* excommunicate. This measure was construed as a personal insult to Edward himself, and a suggestion that his rule was not in accordance with the Charter of Liberties. Edward was much incensed. The very next month he assembled his parliament at Westminster. He forced Peckham to make a humiliating retractation in full parliament of all the canons dealing with Magna Carta and other secular points, which had been passed at Reading in defiance of the rights of the Crown. Not content with this, Edward answered the pretensions of the archbishop with rival pretensions of his own. This parliament passed at the king's instigation the famous Statute of Mortmain.

The Statute of Mortmain was Edward's reply to the Canons of Reading. It was not altogether a new measure, and, as we have already seen, it had a more general aspect in its relation to Edward's constant policy of breaking down class privilege and upholding the legal rights of the feudal lords. But it was, like so much of Edward's work, a real step in advance, though in form largely a definition of previous custom. Its clearness and definiteness make it in essence a startling innovation. It expressly prohibited all future grants of land to ecclesiastical corporations, under penalty of the land thus granted becoming forfeited to the capital lord of the fief. Priests and monks had, in Edward's opinion, land enough already, and it was hard for Peckham, as a Mendicant who believed that the wealth of the Church was at the root of its corruption, to fight with any show of grace against the king's legislation. Still, as an ardent defender of ecclesiastical privilege,

Peckham could not but reckon that a deadly blow had been dealt to the future aggrandisement of the Church.

In 1281 the struggle was renewed. Peckham assembled another provincial council at Lambeth, and again threw down the gauntlet to Edward, by proposing to take all suits concerning patronage and the personal property of clergymen entirely out of the jurisdiction of the king's courts, that he might deal with them in church courts according to canon law. The old question about which Becket had fought so fiercely against Henry II. seemed now on the verge of revival. Edward peremptorily cancelled the proceedings of the council, and again, as in 1279, Peckham yielded to his fierce and uncompromising wrath. In the years that immediately succeeded king and archbishop had a common work to perform against the Welsh; but no sooner was Wales reduced to order than the old disputes were renewed. At last in 1285 a royal ordinance or statute, called *Circumspecte agatis*, was passed, which, while recognising the right of the church courts to deal with suits purely spiritual, rigidly and narrowly defined the limits of the ecclesiastical jurisdiction in matters which had in them a temporal element. With this formal recognition of his rights Peckham had perforce to be contented. Edward came out the real victor in the struggle, though he employed his victory with his customary moderation. But he had been helped by the indiscretion of the archbishop, who, in his zeal for reformation, had raised up for himself a whole host of enemies. Peckham's constant and vexatious metropolitical visitations of his province had excited the liveliest indignation of his suffragans, who saw in his exaggerated estimate of his archiepiscopal powers an attack upon the liberties of every bishop in England. Thus, while Peckham was quarrelling with Edward, the bishops of the southern province were quarrelling with Peckham. So early as the Council of Reading the holy Thomas of Cantilupe had led the resistance to the Franciscan primate. Peckham persecuted him with exceeding vindictiveness, and involved him in costly and vexatious suits at the papal court. When, in 1282, Thomas died in Italy, worn out with asceticism and anxiety, Peckham strove to refuse Christian burial to his remains. Edward showed warm sympathy with the persecuted bishop. He attended the great solemnities which ushered in the translation of the holy bishop's remains to their noble shrine in Hereford Cathedral, where, as men of that age firmly believed, a long series of miracles attested the dead man's claims to sanctity. Edward urged upon the papal Curia that Thomas should be enrolled among the saints, and before his death had secured the appointment of the commission which finally led to his canonisation. Thus did the former Chancellor of Simon de Montfort obtain the honours of sanctity through the victor of Evesham. It was a convincing answer to Peckham's insinuation that Edward did not rule in the spirit of the Great Charter.

Even when most at variance with the archbishop Edward had never failed to respect Peckham's honesty and energy. But as age and ill-success dimmed the activity of Peckham Edward's relations with the Church became easier. For the next few years the king's great complaint was not against the archbishop, but against the greedy popes,

159

whose partisan spirit and lust of strife were the greatest obstacles in the way of his plans for the pacification of the Continent. At home Edward now co-operated with Peckham in a long series of assaults on the Jews.

The Jews had held a strange position in England since the growth of trade, which attended the Norman Conquest, had first attracted them to settle in large numbers in the country. They had accumulated much wealth, owing to their practical monopoly of all banking business; but, as usurers and as infidels, they had made themselves exceedingly unpopular. They were accused of foul crimes, such as murdering and crucifying Christian children, and occasional outbursts of Christian fanaticism had involved them in outrage and massacre. But the Jews had powerful friends. They were the special subjects of the Crown, and were nearly always protected in their usury by the royal officials, on the simple condition that a good share of their spoil found its way to the king's coffers. But as thirty and forty per cent were allowable and moderate rates of interest at this time, the Jews were able to pay great tallages to the king, and still live luxuriously and grow rich. Many of the greater nobles emulated the royal example, and formed an unholy league with the Jews to ruin or buy out their smaller neighbours. During Henry III.'s reign the king's necessities had forced him into constant dependence on the Jews, so that the religious zeal that might, if he had been a free man, have led him in the direction of persecution, found a sufficient outlet in building the Domus Conversorum, a home for converted Jews, on the site of the present Record Office, and in entertaining its few inmates with pensions. As a consequence of this alliance between the Jews and the Crown, the baronial opposition was always strongly opposed to the Jews. In 1215, and again in 1258, the baronial triumph involved the unlucky crown agents in much wanton spoliation and persecution.

Edward disliked the Jews both on religious and economical grounds. The crusading spirit, that had almost lost hope of fighting against the Moslem, saw some satisfaction in wreaking its vengeance on the Israelites. Edward held strongly the mediaeval belief in the sinfulness and harmfulness of usury. He was angry that the Jews fleeced his subjects, and saw with disgust that the lands of an impoverished and spendthrift nobility could hardly render him their due service, because they were mortgaged up to the hilt to Jewish usurers. His own embarrassed finances and constant burden of debt did not make him the more friendly to the money-lender. Early in his reign Edward drew up severe laws, forbidding Jews to hold real property, enjoining on them the wearing of the distinctive and degrading Jewish dress, which was bidding fair to become obsolete, and prohibiting usury altogether. The Jews knew no other way of living, and turned in their distress to even less legitimate methods of earning a livelihood. They sweated and clipped the king's coin so unsparingly that the prices of commodities became disorganised, and foreign merchants shunned a realm whose money standard fluctuated so widely and constantly. In 1278 the royal vengeance came down upon the unlucky sweaters. Nearly three hundred Jews were imprisoned in the Tower on the charge of

161

depreciating the coinage. More than two hundred of them were hanged and their goods confiscated to the Crown. But very few of the Christian goldsmiths and moneyers, who had been the partners of their guilt, were likewise partners in their punishment. Edward caused them to be arrested, but, with a very few exceptions, they were released through the partiality of the Christian juries that tried them.

The lot of the Jews became constantly more grievous. The old charges of murdering Christian children were revived and eagerly believed in. Archbishop Peckham added to the thunders of the State the thunders of the Church. He finally closed up their synagogues altogether, and sternly rebuked Queen Eleanor for suffering her love of money to lead her into unholy alliances with Jews against Christian landowners. But if Edward's wife was lukewarm, his mother Eleanor of Provence, who now played at being a nun, urged on her son to harsh measures against the blasphemers. In 1287, during Edward's long absence abroad, all the Jews in England were imprisoned, and only released on payment of a huge fine. A little later Edward banished the Jews from Guienne. On his return to England, he applied the same policy to his island kingdom. In 1290 he finally expelled the Jews from England. But he allowed them to take with them their movable property, and sternly punished the brutal sailors of the Cinque Ports who had robbed and murdered their Jewish passengers on their way over the Channel. The expulsion of the Jews was a popular act, and the parliament granted Edward a fifteenth as a thank-offering. The king was himself a heavy loser by the transaction, and was thought to have shown rare unselfishness and high religious principle in consenting to get rid of a race so profitable to the royal exchequer. But the Jews were no longer indispensable. Christian usurers from Cahors in Guienne and from northern Italy had deprived them of their monopoly. The Italian agents of Edward's finances were soon as much hated as the Jews themselves had been.

In 1292 Archbishop Peckham died. This time Edward and the monks of Christ Church were in harmony, and Robert Winchelsea, a secular priest and a learned scholastic, but much more a man of action than of letters, was duly elected archbishop. A papal vacancy delayed his consecration, and it was not until 1294 that the new primate entered into complete possession of his office. He at once took up the ultra-clerical policy of Peckham, and combined it with an alliance with every element of secular opposition to the Crown. But the great strife between Edward and Winchelsea, the culminating point in the struggle between Church and State in this reign, can only be properly appreciated in connection with the general history of the latter part of Edward's life. In entering the political sphere Winchelsea was gradually forced into an attitude very different to the purely ecclesiastical standpoint of Peckham.

CHAPTER X

THE SCOTTISH OVERLORDSHIP
1286-1292

DURING the long and peaceful reigns of the second and third Alexanders, the strangely composite territories which make up the modern Scotland had been gradually acquiring unity and national self-consciousness. The western Highlander, the Scot properly so called, had been for centuries joined together with the Pict of the north and north-east. The Welsh of the south-western shires and the English of the Lothians had similarly come into close relationship. The English element had established itself all over the south, and only in the fastnesses of the north or the wild moorlands of Galloway did the old Celtic tongues still continue to be spoken. The silent spread of Norman influence over southern Scotland, in the century succeeding the landing of William the Conqueror, had made the whole nobility of the Lowlands as much and as little French as the nobility of England. Except that the Highlanders retained their lawless old Celtic freedom, and that the Norse settlements, on the Western Isles and the extreme north of the mainland, still kept aloof from their neighbours, the kingdom of Scotland had become a feudal monarchy of the Anglo-Norman pattern, preserving, however, a still stronger Celtic element than the English state, while the newness of any idea of Scottish national feeling, and the weakness of the royal authority, threw greater power into the hands of the nobility and gave less influence to the people at large. The fourfold character of the land—British, Gaelic, Norse, English—still remained, but Scotland was fast settling down into its modern divisions of Highlands and Lowlands. The elaborate process by which Highland chieftains, such as the early Scottish kings were, had become English feudal monarchs had almost been forgotten. The variety of their powers and titles in the various parts of their dominions was rapidly becoming a matter of mere antiquarian curiosity. Even the Norsemen had ceased to look for help to their old Scandinavian homes, after the battle of Largs had put an end for ever to the invasions of the descendants of the ancient Vikings.

The relations between the Scottish kings and the English crown became vaguer as the process of amalgamation went on, and the power of the northern monarchy grew greater. In the old days before the Norman Conquest, there had been countless instances of the Scottish kings acknowledging the English monarch as their father and lord; while the ties which bound them, as lords of Lothian and Strathclyde, to their southern neighbours were undoubtedly still more rigorous and precise. But the feeling that the sovereign's dignity was in some way disparaged by even the most formal acknowledgment of an external overlordship was rapidly extending, and all through the thirteenth century there had been constant bickerings between the English and Scottish kings as to the nature and limitations of the homage, which the former exacted and which the latter in some sort of fashion bestowed.

165

There is, however, little doubt but that the common feeling of the time recognised that the Scottish kings were in a vague way dependent on the English kings, though it is equally clear that it was a supremacy of a very indefinite and old-fashioned sort which brought with it none of those onerous feudal obligations which a potentate so great as the Duke of Guienne paid to his French overlord. The very title of king suggested a greater freedom than this, though the Scottish kings were not in the same rank, according to mediaeval notions, as the greater kings of Europe, who alone received the mystic unction of the Church. It was the height of the ambition of the Welsh princes to vindicate for themselves the substantial position of independence which the Scottish kings enjoyed, despite their nominal subordination to the English crown.

As long as a good personal understanding prevailed between the English and Scottish courts, it was everybody's interest to let sleeping dogs lie. Accordingly Henry III. and Edward I. had contented themselves hitherto with being on good terms with their northern neighbours, and not bringing forward too prominently any unpleasant questions of right. Alexander II. married a daughter of John. Alexander III. married Margaret, a daughter of Henry III., though there was a vigorous national party at his court which sought to ill-treat the young queen as a practical way of protesting against southern influence. Alexander, however, remained firm in his friendship for his father-in-law and brother. If he sent troops to fight for Henry at Lewes, what did it matter that he protested that they were sent by special favour and not as a duty incident to any feudal relations with England? If he protested, on performing homage to Edward, that he saved the rights of his kingdom, it was of little importance to the English king as long as he went through the ceremony publicly and deliberately. Accordingly good peace prevailed between the two realms. But for occasional disturbances on the Borders nothing occurred to break the harmony between the brothers-in-law.

Alexander III. died early in 1286. Margaret of England had already died in 1275, and all her three children had followed her to the grave. The only representative of Alexander and Margaret was their granddaughter, Margaret of Norway, a sickly child scarcely three years old, whose mother, Margaret, the daughter of the King and Queen of Scots, had died in giving her birth, and whose father, a youth still in his teens, was Eric, King of Norway. But the provident care of Alexander had already arranged for the succession of the little Maid of Norway. She was peacefully proclaimed queen, and a commission of regency ruled Scotland in her name. The regents strove, with a moderate measure of success, to put down the disturbances caused by the greedy and unscrupulous nobles, who put forth pretexts to the succession as an excuse for disturbing the realm. Things remained in this condition for nearly three years, when the return of Edward from Gascony to England brought about a new development.

Edward had anxiously watched the progress of Scottish affairs. He resolved that the best way of turning Margaret's succession to the advantage of the two realms, was to negotiate a marriage between the little queen and his only surviving son, Edward of Carnarvon, a boy a few months younger than Margaret. With this object he procured from the pope a bull of dispensation to permit of the union between the cousins, and negotiated dexterously and delicately, both with the regents of Scotland and Eric of Norway. The result was the Treaty of Salisbury, of November 1289, by which the three powers agreed that Margaret was to be sent to Britain before All-Hallowtide 1290, free and unbound by any contract of marriage, while the "good folk of Scotland" gave security that they would make no arrangements for her marriage without Edward's consent. In March 1290 a parliament of Scottish magnates assembled at Brigham on the Borders and solemnly confirmed the Treaty of Salisbury. Edward's success in his first measures led him to take up a more decided line. The excessive caution which kept all mention of Margaret's marriage to Edward out of the Salisbury treaty was now thrown aside. A second set of negotiations were begun at Brigham, the result of which was the Treaty of Brigham of July 1290, in which the marriage between young Edward and Margaret was arranged, and in which King Edward pledged himself and his heirs that, in the event of the match being carried out, the laws, customs, and liberties of Scotland should be for all time observed, and the realm of Scotland should under any circumstances remain "separate and divided and free in itself, without subjection to the realm of England, as has been observed in former times, saving certain ancient rights of Edward over the Marches or elsewhere." The upshot was that, if the crowns became united in the offspring of the union, the kingdoms were to remain separate, while any vague superiority that Edward was still at liberty to claim over the Scots by the terms of the treaty was so whittled away that it could have no practical effects. It was a highly statesmanlike and moderate measure. England abandoned any real overlordship over Scotland that the heirs of the two thrones should unite the kingdoms on equal terms. Very elaborate care was shown to maintain the self-respect of the weaker party, and so to bring about a real and solid union. It had been well for both lands if the Treaty of Brigham had been carried out.

Everything now depended on Edward getting the Maid of Norway into his possession before All Saints' Day. A large and well-equipped Yarmouth ship was despatched to King Eric's court to bring Margaret to her husband and kingdom. So careful was Edward of the little queen's childish wants that a stock of small luxuries—such as walnuts, sugar, ginger, figs, raisins, and gingerbread—was added to the more solid stores provided for the vessel. Norway was safely reached, and in due course the ship of Yarmouth sailed with Margaret from Bergen. But the perils and discomforts of an autumn voyage over the Northern Ocean were too severe for the endurance of the delicate child. She became so ill that the ship put in to the Orkneys to give her relief. But all was in vain. The Maid of Norway died, and with her perished the best hope of a true union of Britain.

The regency continued to rule as before; but its task, hard enough during Margaret's lifetime, became impossible after her death. A swarm of claimants to the throne started up, and sought to prove their rights by an immediate appeal to arms. Anarchy threatened Scotland. It seemed as if the Lowlands were likely to dissolve into a series of petty feudal states like the Lordships Marcher of Wales, for not one of the competitors had strength enough to make head against the others, and there was no strong national feeling to insist upon the maintenance of the unity of the Scottish State.

There was no longer any representative left of the stock of William the Lion, the grandfather of Alexander III. The best claims to the throne were based upon descent from David, Earl of Huntingdon, the brother of King William, and the great-uncle of the last King of Scots. But David himself had left no sons behind him. His heirs were three daughters, whose living representatives were the grandsons of the first and third daughter and the son of the second. It was, however, by no means settled whether females had any right at all over the Scottish succession, so that, apart from the main claimants, a swarm of minor pretenders, representing even bastard branches of the royal family, added to the confusion by pressing forward their fancied rights. Moreover, as regards the claims of the descendants of David of Huntingdon, there were further legal points of great difficulty. John Balliol, the grandson of Margaret, the eldest daughter, demanded the throne as the representative of the senior branch. But Robert Bruce, son of the second daughter, Isabel, claimed to have a better right inasmuch as he was a generation nearer the parent tree than his cousin Balliol. At the same time John Hastings, lord of Abergavenny, a valiant Lord Marcher and a dexterous judge, whom Edward honoured highly, who was the grandson of the youngest daughter of David, argued that the

170

throne should at least be divided according to the ordinary rule of feudal law that co-heiresses had equal shares of the estates that they had inherited. If the kingdom of Scotland was like the earldom of Huntingdon this was no doubt good law. And when the estate was divided among females, the title, unless specially revived, remained in abeyance. But it was not very likely that this doctrine would obtain a favourable hearing in Scotland. It involved an extinction or a division of the kingdom itself. The real dispute then was between Balliol and Bruce, in whose favour most Scots naturally declared themselves; though there was always the danger that the greed of the many claimants should prove too strong for the national abhorrence of the division of the kingdom.

Balliol and Bruce both belonged to the higher feudal aristocracy of Scotland, and both were, characteristically enough, of good north French descent, and at least as much English as Scottish in character, history, and possessions. Balliol was lord of Barnard Castle in Durham, and held by right of his father thirty knights' fees in various parts of England, besides considerable estates in Picardy. He had also by right of his mother, Devorgilla, heiress of Galloway and the pious founder of Balliol College, Oxford, a share in two great inheritances, the half independent lordship of Galloway and the large possessions of David, Earl of Huntingdon. His connection with Scotland was therefore of no long standing, though very considerable. Bruce's family had been settled longer in Scotland, where they ruled over Annandale from their castle of Lochmaben; but Bruce himself had been more occupied during

171

his long and busy career in England than in Scotland, having served for many years as Sheriff of Cumberland and for a time as Chief Justice of the Court of King's Bench. But he was a very old man, and the practical enforcement of his claims lay with his son Robert Bruce, who, by another rich marriage, had acquired the lands and title of the Earls of Carrick. Both the Bruces and Balliols had long aspired to the Scottish succession, and were already on terms of deadly rivalry. Round them the lesser claimants grouped themselves in two fiercely hostile factions.

The regents of Scotland anticipated civil war, and even before Margaret's death the most important of the regents, Bishop Fraser of St. Andrews, had urged that the claimants should peacefully refer their claims to Edward of England. Edward's great moderation and discretion during the Brigham negotiations pre-eminently marked him out as fit to decide so difficult a question. All the claimants agreed to accept Edward as the final judge of their pretensions. The strong sense and clear judgment, which had already arbitrated between the rivalries of Aragonese and Angevins, was now to be brought to bear upon difficulties nearer home. Edward at once accepted the arbitration, and convoked a meeting of the magnates of both realms to assemble at Norham on the Borders on 10th May 1291. Thither there came, side by side with the barons, clerks skilled in the Civil and Canon Laws, and many monks, with the chronicles kept in their respective houses, to instruct the king as to historical precedents for his acts. The assembly met in Norham parish church, where Roger Brabazon, Chief Justice of England, declared that the king had come resolved to do justice to all, and to derogate in no case from the ancient liberties of Scotland. Before, however, Edward would act, he insisted on obtaining from the assembled gathering a recognition of the position, which he now asserted had always belonged to him, as superior lord of Scotland. The Scottish barons were not prepared for so rigorous and sudden a claim, and demanded time for consideration. This Edward granted. The chronicles were consulted and much argument exchanged, but after nearly a month's delay the competitors all accepted Edward's claim, and further agreed that he should have seisin of the land and castles of Scotland until the suit was decided and for two months afterwards. Edward met them half-way by promptly reappointing the former regents, with the addition of one border English baron. The castles were duly surrendered, Edward's peace proclaimed, and the mass of the Scottish barons took oaths of fealty to Edward as their superior lord.

The great suit was appointed to be heard at Berwick, then a Scottish town, and the one great centre of commerce in that poor and disorderly land. A special tribunal was appointed to pronounce judgment, consisting of eighty Scots, of whom Bruce and Balliol each appointed forty, and twenty-four Englishmen chosen by Edward himself. Before the sessions of the great court began, Edward went on a short tour through southern Scotland, visiting Edinburgh, Stirling, Dunfermline, and St. Andrews, and receiving the homages of Scotsmen of every sort, while in places not visited by himself in person his agents did the like. The great court then began its sessions in the castle chapel at Berwick in August 1291. It sat, with frequent and long adjournments, until

173

November 1292. Every point was elaborately investigated, and the strictest regard was paid to the formal law. At last the king's decision was declared in favour of Balliol. Edward rejected the specious but unsound claim of Bruce on account of his greater proximity by blood. He spoke with equal decision against the clever attempt of Hastings to break up the kingdom into three, much as such a course would have helped forward the political interests of England. He declared that the Scottish kingdom was indivisible, and that, both by English and Scots law, John Balliol was the rightful heir of Scotland. The new king was at once put in possession of his kingdom. He was speedily crowned at Scone, and, a few weeks after, performed homage to Edward at Newcastle. Scotland accepted the decision, and for some time King John reigned in peace. All through the great suit Edward's conduct had been thoroughly just and moderate. No one nowadays would deny that his decision was based upon sound law. It was equally sound in policy. If Edward showed a little too much eagerness in taking advantage of the helplessness of the Scots to entrap them into an acknowledgment of his supremacy, it should be remembered that he thought that he was advancing no new claim, but rather one that had been constantly upheld by his predecessors, and supported by plenty of such proof as the vagueness of the relations of the two crowns allowed. He seemed well satisfied, for the pains he had taken in determining the suit, by the unequivocal recognition of his supremacy which he had obtained. If his great scheme for the union of the kingdoms had died with the Maid of Norway, he had at least cleared up and defined wherein his superiority really consisted. Had he gone no further, we should but have had to indicate a new and striking example of his all-embracing policy of definition. As it was, it was but the beginning of a new series of difficulties.

The Scottish arbitration may be looked upon as the culminating point of the power of Edward I. In the eventful twenty years since his accession he had attempted many tasks, but had sought to deal with nothing beyond his strength, and had, allowing for the narrowness of his resources, proved singularly and uniformly successful. He had secured for his people strong and just governance. He had drawn up a great code of epoch-making laws. He had reorganised the finances, and regulated and defined every portion of the constitution. He had annexed and assimilated the turbulent Principality of Wales, and had neutralised the feudal liberties of the unruly Lords Marcher. He had checkmated the great barons, and kept at arm's length the eager and aggressive churchmen. He had secured just limits for Gascony, and reformed its system of government. He had, on both sides of the sea, sought for the good of his subjects, and set up a firm alliance between king and people. He had arbitrated successfully in the greatest European dispute of the day, and had built up a system of alliances which secured his position on the Continent as the great moderating and mediating power. The subjection of Scotland was the crown of a long, a vigorous, and successful career. So strong was Edward's position that Pope Nicolas IV. now again appealed to him to lead the long postponed Crusade against the infidels. Acre had fallen in 1291. Were the princes of Europe to make no effort to recover it, Syria seemed hopelessly given over to Mohammedan rule. For a short time Edward seems to have thought that the hour of the Crusade was come; but before any serious preparations for it had been accomplished, there ensued a period of trial and difficulties, severe enough almost to break down even his dauntless nerve and energy, and from which he had not extricated himself when old age and death at last overtook him.

New scenes are now opened up, and Edward was forced to go on in his work, unaided by the faithful counsellors on whom he had hitherto placed his trust. Between 1290 and 1292 nearly all the chief actors in the earlier part of Edward's reign pass away. Just before the Scottish troubles began, Edward sustained an irreparable loss in his faithful consort Queen Eleanor, who died of some sort of low fever at Harby, near Grantham, in November 1290. "I loved her dearly during her lifetime," wrote Edward; "I shall not cease to love her now that she is dead." Her body was borne with every show of reverence and affection to its last resting-place at Westminster, and Edward's pious care erected a sumptuous tomb over her remains, and a fair cross, a miracle of sculptors' and masons' work, on every spot where her beloved corpse had reposed, on its final sad journey to the Abbey. The chroniclers celebrate her piety, her modesty, her pitifulness, and above all her love for all good Englishmen, and her complete sympathy with the ways of her adopted country. Within a year of her daughter-in-law's decease the less popular Eleanor, Edward's mother, died in her retirement among the nuns of Amesbury, where she had sought to atone for the follies of her past career by a show of entering into religion, without however renouncing those beloved possessions, to obtain which she had incurred so much ill-will among her husband's and son's subjects. But however little Eleanor was beloved by the people, Edward was a good son and deeply felt her loss. Soon after Bishop Burnell, the faithful Chancellor, died, his last public act being the declaration of the king's judgment in the great Scottish suit. John Kirkby, Bishop of Ely and Treasurer, the sharp shrewd financier who served the king so well that he was hated by the people, had already died in 1290. The most famous of Edward's judges had disappeared in the thorough purging of the judicial bench in the same year. And lastly Archbishop Peckham ended his meddlesome and bustling career in 1292, fighting and quarrelling with his clergy down to his dying day. The death-roll of English worthies was, however, trifling as compared with the clean sweep of the older actors on the Continental stage in the years between 1285 and 1292. Both at home and abroad, Edward's later years brought him in contact with another generation, and a generation of meaner stature than that which had gone before. His strong stern figure stands out in increasing loneliness, as his difficulties gathered with his advancing years. So many were his troubles, that we can no longer pursue our former method of dealing with the various aspects of his policy in separate sections. In the critical years which follow, home and foreign affairs, the French war and the Scottish troubles, the strife with the barons and the difficulties with the Church, the constitutional movement and the effort of the king to attain arbitrary power, are all jostled together in hopeless confusion. It is only

177

by examining Edward's action in the midst of so many simultaneous troubles that we can fully realise what manner of man he was.

CHAPTER XI

THE YEARS OF CRISIS
1293-1297

WHILE Edward was successfully establishing his feudal supremacy over Scotland, fresh troubles were brewing between him and his overlord Philip the Fair, who availed himself of a series of petty quarrels between French and Gascon seamen, to press severely against the English king the same claims of superiority, which Edward was now exercising over King John of Scotland.

In the thirteenth century there was no hard and fast line between lawful trade and piracy. The narrow seas swarmed with robber craft, and even in the most peaceful times, seamen and merchants found in the sword the readiest means of satisfying their local rivalries and commercial jealousies. In the course of 1292, the chronic hostility of the Norman and Gascon sailors had assumed a new and fiercer aspect. The Bretons, Flemings, and other seafaring partisans of the French, king backed up the Norman subjects of Philip, while the English and Irish sailors, conspicuous among the former being the men of the Cinque Ports, lent their aid to the Gascon subjects of Edward. Ships were loaded, says a chronicler, not only with merchandise, but with weapons; and though the sea was calm, many a good ship went down, not through being dashed against the rocks, but from the violence of the enemy's

179

attack. At last the Normans gathered together a fleet of two hundred ships, and defiantly sailed through the Channel and Bay of Biscay, hoping that through their immense numbers they would cut off the Gascon wine fleet on its way to England. A fierce sea-fight followed off Saint-Mahé in Brittany, in which fortune favoured the smaller fleet that the Gascons with their English allies had been able to bring together against the Norman Armada. Many French ships with a rich booty were captured, and a vast number of French seamen perished miserably in the fight. The complaints of the defeated crews soon reached the ears of King Philip, who promptly sent to Edward to exact reparation for the injury inflicted by his subjects.

Edward's answer was a characteristic one. The king of England, he said, was a sovereign prince. His courts were subject to no earthly superior. If any man complained of injury done by subjects of the English king, let him come before the English courts with his grievances, and due justice should be done to him. But this high style was mere bravado, for Edward knew quite well that as Duke of Gascony his court had no such sovereignty as he claimed for it. He abated his pretensions so far that he suggested that, if Philip were not contented with the opening of the English courts to his aggrieved subjects, the dispute might be settled by arbitration, or by a personal interview between the two kings.

Philip contemptuously brushed aside all Edward's proposals of compromise, and cited his vassal to appear before his parliament at Paris to answer for the wrongs inflicted by his men on the subjects of his overlord. Edward neglected to appear, whereupon Philip went down in person to the parliament, pronounced the Duke of Aquitaine contumacious, and declared his duchy forfeited for his treason. The Constable of France appeared on the Gascon frontier with sufficient force to execute the royal sentence. A fierce and bloody conflict seemed inevitable.

For more than twenty years Edward had steered clear of a great continental war. He was of no mind to be involved in one at a time when his best efforts were needed to secure his position in Scotland, and when the prospects of leading a Crusade seemed less hopeless than usual. While sending the valiant John of Saint-John with a strong force to protect Gascony from invasion, he still strove by negotiation to avoid the dangers of a long conflict.

Edward sent his brother Edmund of Lancaster to Paris to try and bring about an accommodation. Edmund's wife's daughter was the queen of Philip the Fair, and both she and the widowed queen of Philip the Hardy had powerful influence over Philip. Moreover, Edmund himself had everything to gain by peace, as his wife's dowry in Champagne would inevitably follow the fate of Gascony, were war to be declared. In conjunction with the two queens, Edmund patched up terms of reconciliation, by which Philip's honour was to be satisfied by the surrender of six Gascon castles, and the admittance of one French official into each of the rest of the strong places of Edward's fief as a sign of formal possession, while a proper investigation was to be made, and reasonable compensation offered, for the injuries done by the sailors of Bayonne and Bordeaux to the French. There was further talk of a marriage between the widowed Edward and the French king's sister, which was to be the badge and token of a complete restoration of the ancient friendship.

The six castles were surrendered, and John of Saint-John sold off his military stores and left Gascony. But Philip's ministers were much too astute for the sanguine and confident Earl of Lancaster. The French king now declared, with barefaced treachery, that he had never consented to the arrangements made by the two queens on his behalf. In vain the peers of France backed up the rights of their comrade, the Duke of Aquitaine, against the grasping despot. Gascony was invaded, and as Edward's loyal acceptance of the treaty had deprived him of all means of resistance, the whole duchy passed without so much as a blow being struck into the hands of the French. Edmund in great disgust left his son-in-law's court. Trickery and lying had got the better of straightforward and honest diplomacy. Edward was over-reached, and the war which he had made such sacrifices to avert burst forth with redoubled violence.

Edward now set his diplomatists to work, and soon built up a formidable alliance against the grasping Philip. At the head of this great confederacy was the new king of the Romans, the strenuous but poor and powerless Adolf of Nassau, just raised to the German throne through the unwillingness of the electors to encourage hereditary succession by the choice of the son of Rudolf of Hapsburg. Adolf realised, even more fully than Rudolf had done, the dangers with which French aggression menaced the kingdom of Aries and the whole of those western regions of the Empire, which, with their French tongue and sympathies, were rapidly becoming drawn under the influence of the French crown. The foremost prince of Christendom did not scruple to take the pay of the English king and serve as a mercenary in his hosts. With Adolf came all the princes of the Empire who adhered to his party, having at their head the Archbishop of Cologne. Still closer reasons of fear drew the Netherlandish princes to the English side, including Count Guy of Flanders among the subjects of the French king, and the Counts of Holland and Brabant among the imperial vassals. The heir of Brabant had already been married to one of Edward's daughters, and now another daughter was wedded to the eldest son of the Count of Holland. The still living friendship between Edward and his Savoyard kinsmen gave special importance to the hot championship of the English cause by Count Amadeus the Great of Savoy. Another timely marriage with one of Edward's daughters drew the Count of Bar into the great confederacy. The fierce hatred of the king of Aragon to the French lords of Naples secured him also for the alliance. Philip on his side was scarcely less active, and almost as successful. The dispute about Guienne bade fair to divide Europe into two great camps. Contemporaries were reminded of the old struggle of John of England and Philip Augustus. It was believed that another battle of Bouvines might well be fought.

Edward trusted much to his foreign allies, but he trusted more to the goodwill of his English subjects. These are the years in which Edward's constant recourse to his subjects' pockets brought about, as we have seen, the permanent establishment of the Parliament of the Three Estates. Much indignation was excited by the extraordinary demands which Edward in his supreme necessities laid upon every order of his people. The chroniclers tell us with infinite disgust how the king's officers searched the uttermost corners of the realm for money. They spared neither priest nor monk; they broke open every money-chest; they ransacked the towers and belfries of the churches; and did not even leave unvisited the very lazar-houses where the poorest and wretchedest of the king's subjects dragged out their hopeless and weary life of pain and suffering. Two unpopular classes felt most severely the stress of the national effort. These were the French monks, who fattened on English soil in those "alien priories" which depended on foreign houses of religion; and the foreign merchants, whose debts were collected in the king's name, and whose merchandise was confiscated. But the English clergy, who could not fight, were also expected to exceed all the laity in liberality. The ecclesiastics were at the moment peculiarly defenceless through the vacancies in the papacy and in the archbishopric of Canterbury. Edward at last demanded a half of a whole year's revenue of every beneficed churchman. The unlucky clerks were smitten with terror, and as the king raged and stormed before the assembled convocation, the dean of St. Paul's dropped down dead with fright. By such violence men and money were gathered together, and a general muster was ordered to assemble at Portsmouth in September 1294, whence the army, with the king at its head, was to take ship for

Gascony. But the extraordinary claims of Edward had done something to check his subjects' loyalty. What business was it of plain Englishmen, they might ask, whether Gascony was ruled by Edward or Philip?

The French king's best hopes rested in the disaffection which Edward's strong and imperious policy had excited within Britain itself. His main trust lay in the Scots and the Welsh. King John of Scotland had attended Edward's parliament and promised him help against the French. But even Balliol's sluggish soul had been stirred to indignation by Edward's encouragement of his Scottish subjects to appeal from the decisions of the local courts to the court of the overlord at Westminster. This was a new and unexpected result of Edward's admitted position as feudal superior of Scotland. To Edward it seemed reasonable enough that Scots should appeal to London, just as Gascons appealed to Paris. But to the Scots, who were not litigants, Edward's reception of the appeals clearly gave the lie to his constant declaration that he claimed no rights over Scotland which were not based on ancient custom. On King John's return from the English parliament, he was subjected to the same treatment by the Scottish barons which the parliament of Oxford had imposed on Henry III. in 1258. A council of twelve peers was set up, by whose advice John was for the future to govern. This meant the transference of the government of Scotland into the hands of the worst enemies of Edward's policy. In 1295 a formal alliance was concluded between Scotland and France. It was the first beginning of that memorable connection of Scotland with England's greatest enemy, which inflicted such incalculable mischief upon all Britain for the next three hundred years.

Even before the alliance between the Scots and the French, a threefold revolt had broken out in 1294 in Wales, where discontent with Edward's new arrangements had long been simmering. A partisan named Madog, of the stock of the last Llywelyn, raised the highlands of the north, burnt Carnarvon, and posed as a native prince of Wales. In the southern parts of the Principality, a youth named Maelgwn spread devastation throughout Cardiganshire and Carmarthenshire; while in the great marchland of Glamorgan one Morgan broke out in rebellion against his lord, Earl Gilbert of Gloucester, Edward's son-in-law, and the foremost baron of the realm. With a heavy heart Edward turned away from the Gascon expedition on which he had based all his hopes, and betook himself at the outset of winter to North Wales. The whole work of conquest had to be done over again.

Edward kept his Christmas court at Conway, and afterwards led a winter expedition amidst the snowbound fastnesses of Snowdon. Bands of wild Welsh cut off his convoys. Beer and fresh meat proved wholly lacking, and the fastidious English army had to live, as best it might, on water sweetened with honey, on bread and salt meat. But the Welsh suffered real hardships. As in 1277 and 1283, all supplies were stopped from entering the mountains. By the spring, famine had brought the rebels to their knees, and Edward, having built a new castle at Beaumaris, was able to return to England in May 1295. While he was fighting in Snowdon the great expedition had sailed to recover Gascony under the command of the king's nephew, John of Brittany, who had as his chief councillor the wise and experienced John of Saint-John. At the same time a memorable step was taken in the history of the English navy, by the appointment by Edward of three Admirals charged with the defence of the eastern, southern, and western coasts respectively. The latter division included Ireland, and the Admiral of the West was a valiant Irish knight. It was high time that something was done. The French had begun the war by burning Dover; but the English retaliated by devastating Cherbourg. The Gascon expedition proved a fair success. Its appearance off the coast led to a rising against the French. The loyal fisherfolk and merchants of Bayonne joyfully welcomed back the host of their lawful duke. Bayonne became the centre of a vigorous attempt to win back Gascony; but though some strong places were captured, the greater part of Gascony remained in Philip's hands. Next year (1296) Edmund of Lancaster went to Gascony, but his valour as a soldier could not undo his weakness as a diplomatist. After failing in an attack on Bordeaux, Edmund died of sheer vexation and despair. It was clear both that Edward could not drive out Philip, and that Philip could not expel Edward.

The great northern alliance against France was now the mainstay of Edward's hopes; but as usual in the Middle Ages it was easier to construct an elaborate plan than to carry out a modest one. Very little came of the boasted confederacy. The Count of Holland was murdered and the Count of Flanders changed sides. Many of the great imperial dignitaries thought that they had done their share in the work when

187

they had pocketed Edward's money. King Adolf himself set them a bad example by neglecting his obligations to his English ally and throwing all his scanty strength into a purely personal expedition to the east of Germany. With Adolf's march into Thuringia the last of his grand schemes against French aggression in the Middle Kingdom faded into thin air.

Edward's relations to Scotland partly explain the weakness of the campaign of 1296 on the Continent, and the final failure of Edmund of Lancaster. After forming a close alliance with the French, the Scots rejected all Edward's demands, misused and imprisoned the English merchants at Berwick, and threatened the English border with invasion. For a second time Edward was forced to give up his cherished expedition to the Continent to deal with his foes on British soil. Just as in 1295 the Welsh revolt had prevented him to going in person to Gascony, so now in 1296 he was obliged to betake himself to the Scottish border, leaving his brother Edmund to meet his untimely fate in the south. Balliol had been summoned to appear at Newcastle to justify his conduct before his lord. On his refusal to put in an appearance, Edward got together a great host to invade Scotland, and chastise his contumacious vassal. But Edward had to cope not only with the open hostility of the Scots, but also with the treachery of some of his own subjects. A Welsh knight from Glamorgan, named Turberville, who had been taken prisoner by the French in Guienne, made common cause with his captors and was sent back to England, in name a ransomed prisoner, in reality the agent of a plot against Edward in the French interest. Turberville's plans were detected and he himself was hanged. But he was not the only traitor. A lord of the northern Border called in the Scots to his castle of Wark, and while Edward hurried up to besiege the stronghold of the traitor, seven Scottish earls burst over the western March and spread death and destruction round the walls of Carlisle.

Treason was outwitted and invasion repelled. At last Edward was able to begin his campaign. A goodly host followed the English king over the border. Anthony Bek, the warlike bishop of Durham, called away from foreign diplomacy by the danger to which his Palatinate was exposed, attended Edward's camp with a train of 500 horsemen and 1500 foot. The sacred banner of St. John of Beverley was displayed at the head of the invading army. On 30th March 1296 the great commercial town of Berwick was captured by a sudden and ill-planned but vigorous and persistent assault. A Scottish herald now brought to Edward King John's renunciation of his plighted homage. "The false fool!" cried Edward. "If he will not come to us, we will go to him." Reckless of the havoc which a Scottish invasion of Upper Tyndale was causing in his rear, the king bade his troops press forward. The Scots gathered to withstand the invaders on the heights that surround Dunbar. But on the English approach, they foolishly left their strong position and marched down into the plain, just as the Covenanting army in 1650 delivered themselves in the same way into the hands of Cromwell. On 27th April the van of the English host, under Earl Warenne, fell upon them in their unfavourable quarters and easily scattered them. Next day Dunbar opened its gates to Edward.

The rest of the campaign was but a military promenade. Edinburgh surrendered on 14th June. St. John's day was celebrated within the walls of conquered Perth. On 10th July King John appeared before the bishop of Durham at Brechin and surrendered his person and his kingdom to the English king, bewailing the errors into which he had fallen "through evil counsel and our own simplicity." Edward now pushed on northwards to Aberdeen, whence he marched to the furthermost extremity of the Lowlands at Banff and Elgin. Before the end of August, Edward was back at Berwick. He brought with him the mysterious stone from Scone Abbey, seated upon which the Scottish kings had been wont to be crowned. At Berwick he held a parliament, where those of the Scottish magnates who had not already made their submission vied with each other in performing homage to the conqueror. Few estates were forfeited; no lives were threatened; and no attempt was made to interfere with the ancient laws of the land. The bloodless conquest gave Edward little opportunity of showing his generalship. His fixed resolve to leave things alone in the conquered land was the best proof of his statesmanship. It was a triumph of the most brilliant and unexpected sort. But what probably best pleased Edward at the moment was, that his Scottish conquest at last set him free to try conclusions in person with the hated king of the French. After appointing English officers to rule the Scots, Edward returned to the south, resolved that the forthcoming year should settle the affairs of the Continent, if it lay in mortal power to bring matters to a conclusion.

Despite the fatigues of the campaign Edward allowed himself but little rest. Further supplies were necessary if the king's twice deferred expedition to France were to be a success in 1297. In November 1296 Edward gathered together a parliament at Bury St. Edmunds, and requested large subsidies. The laity made their grant, but the clergy asked for delay that they might deliberate further on the matter. Their debates were long and stormy. The bishops urged upon the priests their obligations as loyal subjects and honourable men. The dignitaries expatiated upon the danger of French invasion. But the proctors of the inferior clergy declared that the purses of the poor parish priests had been drained dry by Edward's previous exactions, and their practical objections to pay anything more were supplemented by the theoretical difficulty which the abbots and priors (the monks were always the strongest papalists) found in the recent action of the pope. Boniface VIII., who had ascended the papal throne in 1294, had issued, early in 1296, his famous bull "Clericis laicos," forbidding clerks to pay taxes to the temporal authority. Archbishop Winchelsea was himself strongly inclined to the view upheld by the monks, but he persuaded the impatient Edward to allow the question to be postponed until January 1297, when a clerical synod was summoned by the Archbishop to St. Paul's in London to further consider the matter. Edward filled up the weary delay by a pilgrimage to Our Lady of Walsingham. The clerical assembly duly met, and after long debates all orders of the clergy united in a point-blank refusal to help the king. Their obligations to Rome had prevailed over their duty to England.

191

Edward was furious with the clergy. "Since you do not observe," he said, "the homage and fealty which you have sworn to me, I too will not be bound to you in anything." He ordered that no clerk should be allowed to sue in the king's courts, and that such of the Church's lands as were held by ordinary lay tenures should be taken into the king's hands. If any layman met a monk or clerk riding a better horse than he had himself, it was declared lawful for him to appropriate it for his own uses. The whole clerical estate was put out of the law. Tidings of a severe defeat of the English in Gascony had come opportunely to hand. In their rage the clergy saw in the disaster to our army the finger of an avenging Providence. But Edward was not so easily turned from his purpose. Archbishop Winchelsea hurried to the king's court to seek to mitigate his sovereign's wrath. On his way the king's officers seized the horses ridden by himself and his followers. Winchelsea got to court as best he could, and found that his intercession was of no avail. Edward gave out that, unless the clergy submitted by Easter, he would confiscate the whole of their lands. Another Church synod met, where love of country and love of gain, fear of the king and fear of the pope, tore asunder the whole order in hopeless divisions. At last Winchelsea was forced to adopt a middle course. He advised each clerk to follow his own conscience, and announced that no ecclesiastical penalty would follow upon submission to the royal will. Most clerks now gladly paid their share of taxation, and were received back into the king's protection. Winchelsea held out obstinately, and Edward took possession of all his lands. The king had thus gained a substantial victory, but only after great friction and a considerable waste of precious months. He never forgave Winchelsea for forcing the conflict upon him and laying clear to all men how divided was the allegiance of the clergy between the pope and the king.

Winchelsea's unpatriotic conduct could have only become successful through the real exhaustion of the tax-payers and the widespread ill-will which Edward's spirited foreign policy had excited. There was no such strong national animosity between France and England as that intense feeling which, in the succeeding century, made it an easy task for Edward's grandson to exact abundant supplies to carry on a war of aggression in France. The laity silently shared in the dislike expressed by the clergy to make Edward further advances; and, just as the dispute with the clerks was approaching settlement, a new difficulty raised by the nobility interposed a further obstacle to Edward's cherished plans.

In February 1297 Edward had assembled a parliament of nobles at Salisbury. He did not summon the clergy, as they were still regarded as outlaws; and he did not convoke the third estate, as the commons had already made their offering at Bury. Edward laid before the nobles a plan of campaign against the French. He proposed to go in person to Flanders in the hope of reviving the energy of the confederate princes, while he requested the leading earls to go to Gascony, where little but Bayonne now remained in English hands. Since the death of Gilbert of Gloucester in 1295, the leadership of the English baronage had passed to Roger Bigod, Earl of Norfolk and Earl Marshal, and Humphrey de Bohun, Earl of Hereford and High Constable. Both earls refused to go to

Gascony, on the ground that they were bound by their offices as Marshal and Constable to attend the king in person. "Willingly," said the Earl Marshal, "will I go with thee, King, and fight before thee in the first line of battle, as I am bound by hereditary duty."—"Thou shalt also go along with the others without me," was Edward's answer. "This I am not bound to do," replied the Marshal; "nor do I intend, my lord, to serve abroad save with thee." Edward burst into a passion. "By God, Sir Earl," he exclaimed, "you shall either go or hang."—"By that same oath, Sir King," answered the Marshal, "I will neither go nor hang." The parliament broke up in disorder. The two earls took arms, and a band of fifteen hundred well-trained horsemen soon gathered together under their banners.

Edward was thus farther off his goal than ever. Despairing of regular grants, he had laid violent hands upon his subjects' goods, and had appropriated all the vast stores of wool and hides which in those days were the only commodities largely produced in England for export. But the followers of the two earls forbade the king's ministers seizing the wool and hides upon their lands, and bade them begone under pain of death or mutilation. Moreover, the townsfolk now began to throw in their lot with the rebellious barons. Nevertheless Edward's fierce will still held out against every obstacle. Inflexible in his great purpose, he ordered a general military levy to assemble at London early in July. But he so worded the writs that it might seem that the military tenants attended, not because bound to appear by reason of their legal obligations, but as a favour at the special request of the king, wailing themselves of this pretext, the Earls of Norfolk and Hereford condescended to appear. With reflection came calmer councils on both sides. Edward appointed other nobles to execute the offices of Marshal and Constable, and the two earls went back to their estates. The king also promised to give pay to all his tenants who served in Flanders, and restored the temporalities of Archbishop Winchelsea and the recalcitrant clergy. On 14th July a formal reconciliation between the king and the archbishop was brought about, in the presence of the king's son, many bishops and barons, and a great multitude of people outside the great hall at Westminster. "For your sakes," declared Edward to his people, "I am going to meet danger. If I return, receive me as you have been wont to do, and I will give you back all that I have taken from you. If I die, here is my son, take him as your king." Winchelsea burst into tears. The people declared their fidelity with uplifted hands. But the touching scene was no sign of hearty reconciliation. The two earls still held aloof; the clergy held long and acrimonious debates as to the precise conditions of their reconciliation; and the Scots burst out into open revolt. The baronial leaders would be content with nothing less than complete submission to their demands, and Edward, after struggling against them for a month longer, resolved to go to Flanders and let English affairs take what course they might. On the eve of his departure he wrote a frank and high-spirited letter to his people, justifying his violent action by his extreme necessity. The heavy taxes and the illegal exactions were as painful to him as to his subjects. He did not impose them to buy lands, or tenements, or castles, or towns for himself, but for the defence of the whole commonwealth against foreign enemies. The whole tone of the letter brings out clearly how Edward valued the opinion of his subjects. Common dangers were still, as in 1295, to be met by common action.

The month of August was nearly over when Edward at last went to New Winchelsea to take ship for Flanders. A few days before his embarkation he had narrowly escaped death from a horse accident. He was riding along the earthen rampart, which then protected the side of the town next the harbour, and which, crowning the brow of a steep hill that sank rapidly towards the sea, gave him an admirable view of his assembled ships. Suddenly the king's horse took fright at the whirr of the sails of a windmill, carried round rapidly by a brisk breeze. The animal refused to stir a step farther, and as Edward plied whip and spur to urge it on, it slipped from the earthen rampart, and fell into the road, many feet beneath, which led down in sharp zig-zags from the town to the harbour. Everybody thought that the king was killed, but the road was soft from recent rain, and the horse miraculously fell on his feet, so that Edward, no worse for his fall, rode back into the town, amidst the rejoicings of the townsfolk and soldiers. He soon afterwards crossed over to Flanders.

No sooner was the king gone abroad than the two earls united with the archbishop in formulating their grievances and demanding redress. On the very day of Edward's departure, the two earls appeared before the Barons of the Exchequer and forbade the collection of the aid until the Charters of Liberties had been confirmed. The regency, at the head of which was the king's son Edward, had neither the means nor the spirit to resist their demands. In a tumultuary and incomplete parliament which assembled in October, the regents reissued Magna Carta and the Charter of the Forests, with additional articles of the utmost importance. By them the recent unlawful aids were utterly renounced, and it was promised that no such taxes should henceforth be levied save by the common consent of the realm, and to the common profit thereof. Next month Edward himself ratified his son's act at Ghent. The long constitutional crisis thus ended for the moment in the complete submission of the king.

The Confirmation of the Charters of 1297 is one of the turning-points in our constitutional history. It sums up the whole advance won by the people in the long struggle, that had raged with but little cessation since the first submission of John to the popular will upon the field of Runnymede. It stands in the closest relation to that development of the parliamentary system which is among the chiefest glories of the reign of Edward. Edward had called into being the parliament of the three estates. By his concessions in 1297, he invested the body that had first met in 1295 with the highest and choicest of its powers. It was the greatest triumph of the popular principle that the age witnessed, and the triumph became all the greater when it was won from so fierce and strong a king as Edward. But the politic submission of the king ended in a fashion the long crisis that had begun with the French king's attack on Gascony. Edward seemed now again set free to carry on his policy as a leader of the English nation. If the last years of his reign—upon which we are now entering—were less glorious than might have been anticipated, it is not because of his concession, but because he did not continue to act in the spirit of his concession; because, while agreeing with his lips to the great principles of popular control and assent, which he himself had enunciated, he acted in his heart in a spirit opposed to them.

CHAPTER XII

THE CONQUEST OF SCOTLAND
1297-1305

THE last few years of Edward's reign were full enough of bitterness to the aged monarch. His disputes with the nobility were only ended by a humiliating renunciation of the dearest prerogatives of the Crown. His attack on France led to nothing better than an unsatisfactory compromise. Even his triumph over the clerical opposition was only obtained as the result of infinite heart-burnings and vexatious personal disputes. If the king's second marriage brought him some measure of domestic happiness, it was more than counterbalanced by the growing certainty that his son Edward was in every way unworthy to succeed to so great a charge as the monarchy of Britain. But all the other troubles of Edward were insignificant as compared with the chronic and growing difficulty of keeping Scotland subdued. He made many sacrifices to get leisure and opportunity to put down the stubborn pride of his Scottish subjects. But one rising was scarcely put down than another burst out. Again and again the thankless work of conquest had to be renewed. And at last the king went down to his grave with the full consciousness that success was farther off than ever.

We have followed the course of Edward's policy in Scotland down to his first conquest of that land in 1296. That conquest had been accomplished with such consummate ease, that Edward very reasonably inferred that it was as final and thorough as his conquest of Wales had been twelve years before. But Scotland was not like Wales. It was not only that it was bigger, stronger, and richer than the western Principality, though these facts in themselves went a long way to explain the difference. In the very divergencies in race and type that Scotland presented, a further explanation of these differences was to be found. Both the Scottish nobles and the Scottish people were made of sterner stuff than the excitable, hot-headed, and disorganised Welsh. It was easy by an appeal to their interests for Edward to obtain a temporary submission from the greedy and self-seeking Norman nobility of Scotland. But the Scots nobles only acknowledged Edward as king so long as they believed that his distant rule would be a nominal rule. Under his guidance they expected to enjoy the turbulent independence of their brethren in Ireland and the Welsh Marches. They had no love for King Edward, though they had a contempt for King John. As soon as they perceived that Edward intended that the conquest should be a real one, they began to manifest symptoms of opposition. They had not signed the Ragman Roll that English ministers should lord it over the land, and ride roughshod over their most cherished liberties. Moreover, behind the politic opposition of the Scottish nobles, there lay the growing sense of indignation of the Scots people. The violent policy of Edward was gradually welding together the sturdy Anglian peasant of the Lothians, the Anglicised Gael of the north-east, and the half-Anglicised Briton of the south-west, into a real and vigorous national unity. As the Norman conquerors of England had fused together Mercian, Northumbrian, and West Saxon by common servitude, so that a single English nation, strong, determined, and united, rose out of the opposition to Angevin despotism, so now the oppressive policy of Edward in Scotland was slowly but surely creating the modern Scottish people. The very fact that the chief formative elements in the new nation were English only added to the severity of the struggle. The Scots, or the most vigorous part of them, shared nearly everything with their would-be conquerors—tongue, institutions, traditions, and character. It was not, truly regarded, a war of two races; it was more properly a civil strife, a great schism of the English race within itself. The struggle was on that account the more stubbornly and persistently fought. And all the statecraft of the great Edward could not reconcile a proud and haughty people to the extinction of its local life.

The fears of the Scots nobles that Edward meant to make himself a real king may have first suggested an opposition to the conqueror. The opposition of the Scottish people to the tyranny of Edward's ministers soon made the struggle an irreconcilable one. As usual Edward was very badly served. Just as twenty years before, all Edward's professions of allowing the Welsh of the Four Cantreds to continue in the enjoyment of their old laws were but a mockery in the face of the misdeeds wrought by a Geoffrey de Langley in Edward's name, so now the English king's protestations that he would rule Scotland justly, after the ancient way, were belied by the greedy vain-gloriousness of a Cressingham and the grim unreasoning severity of an Ormesby. Before long a whole crowd of outlaws and fugitives had been driven by the severity of Edward's ministers to take refuge among the hills and moors. The misgovernment grew worse through the non-residence of Earl Warenne, the king's lieutenant, who shirked the rigours of a northern winter and spring. The outlawed bands came down from their hiding-places and wreaked a bloody revenge on their English oppressors. The rural population welcomed them as deliverers. Before long guerilla forays were exchanged for open warfare. In May 1297 a formidable revolt broke out, headed by William Wallace, whose name (Wallace means simply the Welshman) bespoke his affinity to the old Strathclyde Welsh, and whose gentle birth, gigantic form, iron courage, unbending resolution, and persistent and heroic opposition to the English, to whom, it was believed, he had sworn no oaths of fealty, made him an ideal leader of a revolted nation. The people flocked to his standard with enthusiasm. More slowly and with greater caution many of the nobles and bishops forgot their oaths to Edward, and banded themselves with the national hero. In September Wallace put to flight the English army at Stirling Bridge, and slew Hugh Cressingham, the worst of the oppressors. Next month the victorious partisan dashed over the borders and harried Cumberland and Westmorland. Earl Warenne, recalled to his post by the rebellion, was powerless to withstand the mighty rush of the popular wave. Scotland was freed from end to end. The rule of the English earl had been succeeded by the government of William Wallace and Andrew Murray, "the generals of the army of the kingdom of Scotland" and the wardens of the absent King John.

While the Scots insurrection was running its course, Edward was still occupied in Flanders, whither he had taken a large army of Englishmen and Welshmen. But he made no way against the French, and was involved in all sorts of difficulties with his allies. Philip the Fair burst into Flanders, captured Lille, and occupied Bruges. The conquest of Bruges cut off Edward, who was at Ghent, from the sea. A vigorous attack was therefore ordered to be made upon the French positions. The French were almost defeated, when the two wings of the ill-assorted allied army destroyed by their mutual animosities the hope of victory. The Flemings fought so fiercely with the English and Welsh about the booty that the day was lost.

Boniface VIII. now offered his mediation. Both Edward and Philip were averse to recognising any right of the pope to interfere in his official capacity in the disputes of sovereign and independent princes; but both wished to end the struggle, and agreed, while rejecting the proposals of the pope, to accept the friendly offers of the man, Benedict of Gaeta, who then filled the papal throne. A two years' truce was patched up, which finally ripened into a definite peace.

After the truce was signed, there arose a violent dispute between Edward's turbulent soldiers, largely Welsh and Irish, and the townsmen of Ghent. It culminated in a two days' pitched battle in the streets, during which Edward was exposed to considerable personal risk. Extricated from this trouble by the strenuous efforts of Count Guy, Edward had now leisure to return to Britain, where his presence was sorely needed. In March 1298 he landed in his kingdom, and at once busied himself with preparations for an expedition to suppress the revolt of Wallace. He held a hasty parliament at York, but the Scots lords, to whom summonses had been sent as well as to the English peers, unanimously disregarded his commands. The feudal levies were then summoned to meet at Roxburgh, a strong Scottish fortress that still remained in English hands. Edward piously prepared himself for his work of conquest by a pilgrimage to his favourite shrine of St. John of Beverley. On Midsummer Day the English host mustered at Roxburgh. There was a splendid array of heavily armed knights and men-at-arms, all mounted on horseback. Edward, who was in many ways an old-fashioned soldier, regarded the feudal cavalry as the real strength of an army, and on this occasion he had so little concern of the infantry that he only enforced the attendance of those who were bound to serve on horseback. Nevertheless, a large number of volunteers served on foot, nearly all of them being Welsh and Irish. But the gallant show was far from unanimous or whole-hearted. The Earls of Norfolk and Hereford refused to fight unless the king again confirmed the Charters. But the Bishop of Durham and the Earls of Lincoln and Warenne pledged their word that if the king came back victorious he would do what the two earls required.

The English host now advanced into Scotland. Wallace had retired beyond the Forth, and no opposition was offered to Edward's advance to Edinburgh, whither the army went on slowly, plundering and devastating the country on the line of route. Having taken possession of the capital, Edward marched westwards as far as Kirkliston, a village on the borders of Mid- and West-Lothian, where he made a long halt. It was dangerous to advance farther until Dirleton Castle, between Edinburgh and Dunbar, which was strongly held by the Scots, had been captured; and when the warlike Bishop of Durham at last succeeded in this task, there were such grave difficulties in provisioning the army that Edward was still forced to remain stationary at Kirkliston. A contrary wind prevented the provision ships from sailing up the Forth, and the only vessel that arrived had a large cargo of wine which, by Edward's orders, was distributed among the soldiers. The irregular Welsh infantry had suffered most from the lack of victuals, and were dying off in large numbers; but Edward now sent such a bountiful supply of wine to revive their spirits that they all got drunk. A quarrel broke out between the Welsh and the English men-at-arms. The Welsh slew eighteen Englishmen, but the English retaliated, killing a large number of Welshmen and putting the rest to flight. The Welsh now talked of joining the Scots. Edward professed to set little store on their action either way. "What does it matter," he said, "if enemies join with enemies. Welsh and Scots are alike our enemies. Let them go where they like, for, with God's blessing, we shall in one day obtain our revenge over both nations." But the lack of victuals continued, and on 21st July Edward gave orders to retreat to Edinburgh. At that moment a boy brought the news that Wallace, having marched to within six leagues on the English, was encamped at Falkirk, and proposed to follow the English up on their retreat to Edinburgh and to surprise their camp on the following night. "As the Lord lives," cried Edward, "there will be no need for them to follow me, for on this very day I will march forward and meet them face to face." He at once ordered the English army to advance to Linlithgow, where it encamped in the presence of the enemy on the open heath. That night was an anxious one in the English camp. The prospect of battle had again reconciled the Welsh and English, and every man slept as best he might with his shield as his only pillow and his armour as his bedclothes, while the horses, kept ready for action by their masters' sides, had nothing to taste but the hard steel of their bits. In the midst of the night a wild cry arose in the English ranks. Every one believed that the enemy was at hand. But all that had happened was that the horse of the king, tethered like that of the meanest trooper to his rider's side, had trodden upon the sleeping Edward and broken two of his ribs. But when day dawned the king mounted his horse as if nothing had happened, and marshalled his troops for the great battle that was at hand.

It was the 22nd July, the feast of St. Mary Magdalen. At early dawn the English marched through the streets of Linlithgow, and saw the Scots lances glistening on the crest of a neighbouring hill. But when the English advanced, the enemy retreated to a remoter and stronger situation. A halt was therefore ordered, and mass was said before the king and bishop. The English then advanced against the army of Wallace, now drawn up to meet their attack.

The generals of this period placed all their trust in the heavy armed feudal cavalry, but with half the Scots nobles still waiting upon events, there was but a scanty muster of horsemen among the insurgent host, and Wallace was forced to rely on the foot folk that constituted the mass of his army. The great danger to infantry was lest they should be swept away and overwhelmed in the fierce rush of a heavy armed cavalry charge. To prevent this Wallace hit upon a novel plan, the conception of which shows him to have had the making of a great general in him, and strikingly anticipates Wellington's tactics at Waterloo. He drew his pikemen up in four great squares or circles in close formation, and with palisades to further strengthen their ranks. A morass protected their front; archers filled up the gaps between the squares; and a scanty corps of mounted knights formed a rear guard. It was a strange order of battle, and nothing like it had been seen in Britain since the cavalry of William the Norman had scattered the foot folk of Harold on the hill of Hastings. An English poet describes vigorously enough the strange scene:—

"There speres poynt over poynt, so sare and so thikke.
And fast togidere joynt, to se it was verlike,
As a castelle thei stode that were walled with stone,
Thei wende no man of blode though tham suld haf gone."

As Wallace contemplated the novel array, he exclaimed triumphantly, "I half brocht you to the ring, hop gif ye can." But though the Scottish partisan had conceived the possibility of resisting cavalry by closely trained infantry planted in a compact mass, he was not destined to see the triumph of a system which within a generation was to revolutionise the art of warfare. The Scots at Falkirk did not succeed as the Flemings at Courtrai, the Swiss at Morgarten, and the very Scots themselves at

Bannockburn, succeeded in withstanding the fierce rush of the line of mail-clad warriors on their mail-clad steeds. The main reason for this was to be found in the generalship of Edward, who while adhering in the main to the old-fashioned tactics of a cavalry charge, had skill enough to modify them in such a way as to meet the new danger involved in Wallace's formation. In three great "battles" or divisions, Edward poured his host on to the Scots army. The first line stuck in the morass and fell into some confusion, but the second line wheeled about and vigorously assailed the enemy in flank. The scanty Scots horse galloped away in a panic. Their numbers were much too few to make resistance possible. But their withdrawal compelled the Scots archers also to seek safety in flight. This left the four squares to bear the whole brunt of Edward's attack. For some time the serried masses of pikemen held their own gallantly behind their palisades. Edward saw that there was no prospect of breaking through their ranks by the mere momentum of a cavalry charge; he therefore poured in showers of arrows upon the squares, and before long the deadly hail began to have its effect. Gaps were soon made in the ranks, through which the English knights galloped in. With the breaking up of their ranks the Scots army was turned into a mob of fugitives. The light armed Welsh and Irish footmen reaped the spoils of the victory. While heavy loss was inflicted on the Scots, only two knights and a few of the "common folk" fell on the English side. Wallace fled, and soon withdrew from the country. His short strange career of generalship ended as suddenly as it had begun. This is the more wonderful as Edward reaped no very great results from

208

his brilliant victory at Falkirk. He consumed a fortnight inactively at Stirling, while his broken ribs grew together again. Lack of victuals prevented an advance beyond Perth, and compelled the abandonment of all thoughts of a conquest of the Highlands. Edward on his recovery resolved on the conquest of the south-west, where Robert Bruce, the young son of the cautious Earl of Carrick, and the grandson of the competitor, held the chief power and strove to secure his own independence with little care for either side. But provisions were still harder to find upon the barren moors of Galloway than in the fair corn-fields and pastures of the Lothians. September saw Edward back at Carlisle. Despite his great victory, the conquest of Scotland had hardly been begun. Operations for the year were perforce suspended, when the selfish policy of Norfolk and Hereford insisted on an immediate return to their homes.

For nearly six years Edward strove to complete that conquest of Scotland which he had begun by his victory at Falkirk. Year after year he entered Scotland, and little by little the stubborn Scots bent their backs to the English yoke. The courts of justice and the apparatus of government were transferred from London to York, and it seemed as if the old Roman city was again about to become the permanent capital of a united Britain. But all sorts of difficulties still stood in Edward's way. He still had to deal with the persistent agitation of his subjects for the renewal of the Confirmation of the Charters. He had still to conclude his intricate negotiations with the French king. He did not establish any real understanding with his subjects until 1301. His French troubles were not finally over until 1303.

The peace with France involved both delays and difficulties. The truce was turned into a formal peace, which was signed at the famous Cistercian Abbey of L'Aumône in the Chartres country in the summer of 1299. In accordance with its provisions Edward was married to Philip's sister Margaret, and his son Edward promised to Isabella, Philip's daughter. In return for this Edward tacitly abandoned his Flemish allies to the vengeance of the French king, though the Flemings declared that in so doing he broke an oath which he had sworn to Count Guy. But Edward was seldom over-scrupulous, and his real object was to get from Philip a similar abandonment of the Scots. Against this his brother-in-law long held out, and on various pretexts still kept Gascony in his hands, but in 1302 the stubborn Flemings utterly defeated the chivalry of France in the famous battle of Courtrai, where the tactics with which Wallace had failed to win the day at Falkirk, were repeated with overwhelming effect against the best cavalry of Christendom. Philip now saw that he had plenty of work cut out for him at home, especially as his old strife with Boniface VIII. had been recently renewed in a more inveterate and deadly form, and Boniface, changing his policy, strove to induce Edward to renew his attack on Philip. But Edward was of no mind to serve the pope's turn, the more so as Philip, induced by necessity, now gave way about the Scots. In 1303 a definitive peace was signed between France and England; Gascony was restored, and an offensive and defensive alliance entered upon by the two kings. For the rest of his reign Edward remained at peace with the nations of the Continent. His persistency had in the long run overcome the duplicity of his neighbour. The struggle for the mastery in Britain could now be fought out on British soil unhindered by foreign intervention.

The constitutional struggle was much harder to settle. The Confirmation of the Charters in 1297 proved not the end, but the beginning of a new and acrimonious controversy between the king and his subjects. The two earls were not satisfied with Edward's first ratification of his son's acts, and their hesitation to discharge their obligations against the Scots, unless Edward again confirmed the Charters, was, as we have seen, a source of weakness to the king all through the Falkirk campaign. Next year (1299) the demand for the further confirmation both of the Great Charter and of the Forest Charter was again raised. But, like a true descendant of the Norman kings, Edward regarded the forests as the special property of the crown and resented all restriction of his forest rights as an insult both to his person and to his dignity. He was forced indeed to give way, but the blessings of the people were changed into curses when it was found that he had confirmed the Forest Charter with the proviso "saving the rights of the crown." A long agitation now broke out, during which neither side showed much temper or forbearance. Edward's evident reluctance to yield up any tittle of his prerogative, and his strong tendency to interpret any concession he made, in the narrowest and most technical spirit, added to the exasperation of his subjects; while the old king grew

211

beside himself with fury when he found his barons and parliaments perfectly indifferent to the progress of his Scottish conquest, and persistently refusing all help except on the terms of his complete submission. Very reluctantly and unwillingly, Edward yielded to the inevitable in the parliament of 1300, and by the issue of the *Articuli super Cartas* evaded a formal confirmation by accepting in another way the main conditions imposed on him by his subjects. But even then he had no peace. In 1301 a new parliament assembled at Lincoln, where a clever combination against the king was carried through by the dexterous diplomacy of Archbishop Winchelsea. The estates demanded the removal of the treasurer Walter Langton, Bishop of Lichfield, and the chief minister of Edward's later years. Again Edward was forced to an almost unconditional submission, through which he saved his minister. After all the Scots war lay nearest to his heart, and he at length saw that, as long as king and people were divided, the Scots could never be subdued.

Edward had made great concessions both to France and to his parliaments, in order to isolate the Scots from all moral and material support. But a third obstacle now interposed itself between him and his revolted subjects in a peremptory order from Boniface VIII. that Edward should desist from the Scots war. Scotland, said the pope, was a fief of the Holy See. To wage war against the Scots was to rob the papacy of its choicest prerogative of protecting its obedient subjects. The claim was first put before Edward while on his Scots campaign. Winchelsea was, as usual, on the pope's side. He now sought out the king in Galloway with a papal envoy in his train. Edward's hot temper fired up as the archbishop exhorted him in Biblical phrase to desist from further hostilities. "By God's blood," he cried, "I will not hold my peace for Sion, nor keep silence for Jerusalem; but I will maintain my right, which all the world knows, with all my might." In the Lincoln parliament, Winchelsea was again active in pressing the pope's claim. But the barons, though they joined with the archbishop in his demand for the confirmation of the Charters, stood manfully by the king in resisting this new and unheard-of papal pretension. A spirited remonstrance was drawn up in the name of the barons, which declared in good round terms that the pope's interference was meddlesome and intolerable. The result was that the relations between England and Rome again became strained. As a further result, Boniface's attitude left Edward in no mood to listen to the entreaties of the pope to take up his side in the great struggle that now broke out between France and the papacy. Edward was too pious, and too busy at home, to join actively in Philip's violent and brutal onslaughts on the unhappy pope. But the fall and death of Boniface in 1303, and the thorough subjection of the papacy to France which followed, taught Edward to estimate at their true value the thunders of Rome. He was at last free from papal as from baronial and foreign opposition.

During the weary years of threefold strife, Edward had still turned his whole available energies to the reconquest of Scotland, though he had made little progress. In 1299 the barons had refused to follow him, as his promises to keep the Charters were still unratified. After his submission in 1300, Edward was able to take the field with a gallant army, that marched from Carlisle to the conquest of the south-west. The most famous incident in this campaign was the capture of Carlaverock, a stronghold held by only sixty men against Edward's great host, and commemorated in a French poem, dear to genealogists and heralds. In 1301 Edward was again in Scotland, and, after conquering the greater part of the lands south of the Forth, he took up his winter quarters in the old palace of the Scots kings at Linlithgow. Early in 1302 Edward held a "Round Table" at Falkirk to celebrate the progress of his conquest. But though the Scots yielded before the advance of his troops, they were still far from being subdued. In 1302 the Scots surprised and defeated the king's troops at the battle of Roslin. This was their last great success.

In 1303 the real conquest of Scotland began. Edward was at last free to devote all his energy to the task, and long years of warfare had worn out the energies of the long-suffering Scots. Edward's work now seemed quite a simple one. Edward next made a great progress throughout Scotland, which recalls the famous march in 1296. He marched through Perth, Brechin, and Aberdeen to Banff. As far north as Caithness the weight of his arm was felt, and the Highland chieftains flocked to his camp to make their submission. At last John Comyn, who had governed Scotland since Falkirk as regent for King John, despaired of further resistance and made his peace with Edward. The only strong place that now held out was Stirling. Edward took up his winter quarters at Dunfermline, where (so peaceful was the country now) he was joined by his young queen. With the spring of 1304 the attack on Stirling began. It was a siege conducted with all the military skill known at the time. Huge wooden machines cast stones weighing two or three hundredweight into the castle. Batteringrams were brought to bear against the walls. Movable turrets were wheeled up against the battlements, and the fosses were filled up with stones and earth. At last, on 20th July, the scanty garrison surrendered. There was no longer any organised resistance to Edward's authority in Scotland. But Wallace, the hero of the first revolt, who had almost disappeared from history after his defeat at Falkirk, now again came on the scene. His old fame was half forgotten, and the long struggle had disheartened the Scots too much for them to venture upon a fresh rising. The hero lurked in the woods and hills with a scanty following, while Edward, secure of his triumph, returned to England, and, as a sign that the war was over, ordered the return of the courts of justice and officers of state from York to Westminster. Nor was the king's confidence ill-grounded. In the summer of 1305, Wallace was captured through the treachery of a Scot, and brought to London for trial. Condemned as traitor, murderer, and incendiary, Wallace suffered in due course the terrible penalties of the English law of treason. His death has been made a matter of reproach to Edward, on the ground that, unlike most of his countrymen, he had never become the king's vassal; but the evidence of this fact is not very good. Moreover the laws of war were stern in the fourteenth century, and no technical claim of right was likely to protect the very soul of the long resistance of Scotland. Edward acted as any one else would have acted in his place. In holding out against Edward, Wallace knew full well that he carried his life in his hands. It adds rather than lessens the glory of the Scottish hero that in due course he paid the penalty of his heroism and self-devotion. But the special glory of Wallace belongs to a later age, when the songs of the Scottish bards had made him the popular hero of the war of independence.

Edward now drew up a scheme for the government of Scotland. An English parliament met in September 1305 to settle the question. In this assembly, Edward, true to his doctrine of popular control, caused ten representatives of the Scottish estates to appear. These included two bishops, two earls, two abbots, two barons, and two representatives of the commons, one for the north and the other for the south. A committee of twenty English lords was associated with the Scots members to draw up a scheme. From their joint deliberations sprang the "Ordinance for the Government of Scotland," the last and perhaps the most striking of Edward's many claims to statesmanship.

Admitting that Scotland was to be ruled by Edward at all, it is hard to see how the government of Scotland could have been better arranged than by this plan. John of Brittany, Edward's faithful nephew, was made warden or lieutenant of the whole land, with the ordinary officers of state under him. For the purposes of justice Scotland, like Wales, was divided into large districts. Eight judges were chosen—two for the Lothians and the other English lands south of the Forth, two for the Welsh or British lands of Galloway and Strathclyde, two for the English-speaking lands between the Forth and the Grampians, and two for the Celtic Highlands. Sheriffs, coroners, and the other officers of the English shire system, were appointed to hold office during the king's pleasure. They were to be either Englishmen or Scotsmen. The rude Celtic laws—the laws of the Brets or Welsh in Strathclyde, and the laws of the Scots or Highlanders—were, like the Welsh laws of Howel Dda, repugnant to Edward's notions of justice. They were therefore to be swept away, and replaced by the English and Norman laws which, since the days of King David, had prevailed in the Scottish Lowlands. John of Brittany was instructed to assemble the "good folk of the land "of Scotland in some fixed place and ascertain from them what King David's laws really were, and what additions had been subsequently made to them. He was also directed to redress and amend such of the Scots laws as are "plainly against God and reason," taking the advice of both English and Scottish councillors in arriving at this result, and referring all decisions of great importance to the immediate judgment of the King of England. Thus by Edward's scheme a separate administration was provided for Scotland, though the Scots were secured with some measure of representation in the English parliament. For the most part the Scots administration was put into Scots hands; and the prospect of a great legislative reform in the immediate future was an additional inducement for the Scots to accept the new constitution, with its programme of practical reforms and strong sound rule, as a substitute for their old turbulent independence. But it was too late for conciliation. Nearly twenty years of warfare and hatred had worked out their fateful results. Nothing but sheer force

217

kept Scotland obedient to her foreign conqueror. Half Scotland waited for an opportunity for rebellion. That opportunity was not long in coming.

CHAPTER XIII

THE END OF THE REIGN
1305-1307

WITH Scotland subdued and apparently appeased, Edward was again able to turn his mind to English affairs. He was a man slow to forgive and tenacious in his policy. He had neither forgotten nor forgiven the humiliations inflicted upon him by the union of the baronial and clerical opposition in the years between 1297 and 1301. He still chafed at the restraints then imposed upon his prerogative, and his pious fear of breaking the oath he had so unwillingly sworn only added to his restlessness and uneasiness. The baronial opposition was already broken up. Hereford died in 1298, and Norfolk had completely abased himself by a temporary surrender of his estates to the crown, and by receiving them back, fettered with the obligations of a conditional estate that came under the provisions of the Statute *Quia Emptores*. Edward was thus in a position to carry out a policy which he had devised to prevent a renewal of the baronial opposition. His greatest danger was from the higher aristocracy represented by the great earls. The earldom of the days of Edward stood in a very different position to the somewhat commonplace dignity which goes by the same name in the nineteenth century. The earldom was still the highest rank of the peerage. It still retained some traces of its earlier position as the official head of a

219

county. It involved a great position both in the court and in the nation. The number of earls was so scanty that each individual earl was personally and territorially important. In the earls the people saw their natural leaders.

Edward's plan seems to have been to prevent a renewal of the baronial opposition, and to add to the strength of the crown by getting as many of the great fiefs as he could under his direct control. Circumstances favoured his design, and a series of lucky escheats and well-designed marriages much facilitated the process. In 1300 the death of Edward's cousin, Edmund of Almaine, threw the rich earldom of Cornwall into the king's hands. On the death of the Earl of Norfolk in 1306 his earldom also escheated to the crown for lack of heirs to his body. Contemporary writers put Edward's lucky acquisition of these two great earldoms side by side with his conquests of Wales and Scotland. The young Earl Humphrey of Hereford married in 1302 the king's daughter Elizabeth the Welshwoman, the widowed Countess of Holland. Meanwhile former efforts in the same direction were bearing fruit. Joan of Acre administered the Gloucester inheritance of Edward's youthful grandson. The young Thomas of Lancaster, Derby, and Leicester was expecting the succession of Lincoln and Salisbury. Edward of Carnarvon now ruled over Wales and the earldom of Chester. Edward and his near kin thus enjoyed a remarkable concentration of the great earldoms in their hands. The policy had a temporary success, and perhaps accounts in part for the cessation of the baronial opposition in the last years of Edward's reign. But the policy had its dangerous side, and its permanent results were by no means favourable either to the dignity of the crown or to the prosperity of the nation. The chroniclers attribute the decadence that set in after Edward's death to the dying out of so many of the old earldoms. Still Edward's policy was at least a thoroughly English policy, and if it failed, it failed largely because, by identifying the younger branches of the royal house with the ancient feudal dynasties, it also identified them with the hereditary jealousies and factions of the old lines of earls. It had the merit of making impossible a royal caste, cut off by rigid laws of etiquette and pride of birth from the general mass of the nobility. It was both the strength and the weakness of Edward, that while he was politically but the greatest official in the kingdom, he was socially but the head of the English aristocracy. Though he firmly believed that his power was of God, he never aspired to be the semi-divine ruler, set by his birth and position upon a pedestal that kept him solitary and apart from the life of the country over which he ruled.

The baronial opposition being thus got rid of, the clerical opposition alone remained to be dealt with. Winchelsea was still unreconciled. But Winchelsea held a great position and could not easily be attacked. Since the Falkirk campaign Bishop Bek of Durham had, to Edward's intense disgust, thrown up his diplomatic and military positions, and, after a vain attempt at mediation, allied himself to Winchelsea. But Bek got mixed up in obscure struggles with his chapter, and, on his setting out for Rome in 1302 without the king's permission, Edward took into his own hands the rich temporalities of his see. On his return, Bek submitted himself to Edward, who restored him his lands. But fresh difficulties soon drove Bek back to the papal court, where he obtained in 1305 the sounding title of Patriarch of Jerusalem. Edward complained that he had obtained from the pope grants injurious to the rights of the crown, took away from him some of his best manors, and never left him in peace for the rest of his life. When Edward pursued Bek, with whom he had no personal quarrel, with such unremitting rancour, it was plain that he was only waiting his opportunity to inflict an even more signal vengeance on the hated archbishop.

In 1305 the favour of Philip the Fair secured the papacy for Edward's Gascon subject, Bertrand de Goth, Archbishop of Bordeaux, who assumed the name of Clement V. As evidence of his subservience to the French king, Clement now transferred the seat of the papacy from Italy to France, and began that fatal seventy years of Babylonish Captivity, which did so much to lower the Holy See, both in actual power and popular esteem. Clement showed almost as much deference to Edward as to Philip. His submissive attitude gave opportunity for Edward to work out a great plan of revenge, while it encouraged king and nation alike to enter into a course of anti Roman legislation that was England's revenge for Pope Boniface's slights upon her independence.

Edward still fretted under his obligations to observe the Charters. As soon as Clement had become pope, he applied for and obtained a dispensation from his oath to observe the Charters in their new and enlarged form. The complaisant pope at once gave the required absolution, and Edward issued a new Ordinance of the Forest in which he repudiated those portions of the revised Forest Charter which had so long offended his sense of dignity. Further action he did not take, and this must be considered a sign of moderation, for Clement's bull was so wide in its wording that it would have empowered Edward, if he had a mind to it, to repudiate the whole of the additions to the Great Charter wrung from him in 1297. This shows that Edward had no design of violating the essential elements of the English constitution, but it was at best a great falling away for the old king to revert to the worst precedents of his stormy youth. This declension from the doctrine of "keep troth" may tend to take the king off the lofty pedestal on which his admirers have sometimes placed him. But nothing was more natural for a mediaeval king, than to submit his conscience to his interests, and in no way did the papacy exercise a more demoralising influence upon Europe, than through the facility with which it gave men of easy or formal honesty a means of sheltering their weakness under the protecting aegis of the Church.

The king's vengeance was now turned on the able and accomplished primate, whose rigid regard for the interests of his cloth and persistent hostility to the crown were now to be atoned for by a signal fall. Winchelsea's relations with Edward had been further complicated by a fierce and unworthy quarrel with Edward's favourite minister, Bishop Walter Langton. The archbishop had accused Langton of simony, adultery, murder, and intercourse with the devil; but the minister had been triumphantly acquitted of these foul and monstrous charges, and now pursued the primate with a deadly hatred. A long accusation was sent up to Avignon against Winchelsea, of which the most serious part was a charge of treason, based upon his conduct in the parliament of Lincoln in 1301. Clement again showed the utmost willingness to oblige the king. Winchelsea was suspended and summoned to appear before the papal court. In a last stormy interview the archbishop besought the king for leave to quit his kingdom. "Permission to go," said Edward, "right willingly we give, but permission to return thou shalt never have. We know thy craft, thy subtlety, thy treachery, and thy treason. The pope will deal with thee as thou deservest. Favour at our hands thou must never expect. Merciless hast thou been to others, mercy to thyself will we never show." Edward was as good as his word, and for the rest of his reign Winchelsea remained in poverty and exile. But Edward quickly quarrelled with the complaisant pope on the question of the administration of the lapsed revenues of the see of Canterbury, and Edward was fully backed up by the rising anti-papal feeling in the nation. The spirit which had animated the barons at Lincoln culminated in 1307 in the famous Statute of Carlisle, the first act of anti-Roman legislation in England. Nothing but Edward's death prevented a regular breach with the pope.

Never did Edward's affairs seem more flourishing than in the early part of 1306. Scotland remained subdued; the French were friendly; the pope was the king's creature; the barons and commons were alike well disposed; the arch-enemy Winchelsea was in exile. Though old and stiff, Edward remained in good health. He had recently taken vigorous steps to grapple with the administrative disorder which was almost chronic in the Middle Ages, and nothing had made the old king better liked among peace-loving men than his putting down, by his writs of *trailbaston*, the groups of armed ruffians who worked all sorts of misdeeds. The only drop of bitterness in the cup of his happiness was the unworthy conduct of his son and heir. Immense pains had been taken to instruct the young Edward in martial accomplishments, and drill him in the principles and routine of business and statecraft. But within the tall, strong, handsome frame of the young prince was the heart of a coward and trifler. He had no serious interests, wasted his time in gambling and rioting in low society, and cared for nothing but his horses, hounds, players, and boon companions. In 1305 the young Edward had incurred his father's ire by a wanton attack upon Bishop Langton, and was with difficulty restored to favour by the good offices of his stepmother. The certainty that there was no guarantee that his policy should be continued after his death must have weighed heavily upon the aged king.

Terrible news now came from Scotland. Robert Bruce, the grandson of the claimant, Earl of Carrick since 1304: by his father's death, had for several years been among Edward's Scottish partisans. But he now withdrew himself from the court and took horse for Scotland, where on 10th February 1306 he met John Comyn, the former regent, in the Franciscan Convent at Dumfries. The two men were old rivals, the representatives of houses long hostile to each other. A dispute broke out. Hot words passed. Swords were drawn, and Comyn was slain. Bruce was now forced to become a fugitive, and in self-defence was compelled to identify himself with the party of Scottish independence, with which in recent years he had been secretly intriguing. He found that the spirit of Scottish nationality still burnt as fiercely as ever. He soon manifested a skill and daring that shows him to have been a born leader of men. Before Lent was out, half Scotland was again in revolt. On 25th March Bruce was crowned King of Scots at Scone. A few strong castles with their English garrisons, and a few nobles jealous of Bruce's progress, alone actively upheld the English cause.

The ill-tidings of the Scottish revolt were brought to Edward at Winchester, whither he had gone to keep his Lenten court. He burst into a terrible explosion of wrath, and resolved to stamp out all resistance in the stubborn and intractable nation on which all clemency was thrown away. Troops were at once despatched to the north, and a great gathering of the younger nobles was summoned to Westminster to prepare for an expedition of crushing numbers and force. The king was now so infirm that he could not ride, and was taken from Winchester to London in a horse-litter. On Whitsunday he held a gorgeous pageant at Westminster. He solemnly dubbed his son Edward a knight. Three hundred young men of noble houses gathered together in the Abbey Church to receive the same honour from their future king. There was such a pressure round the high altar of the Abbey that two of the new knights were crushed to death by the throng. Then two swans, their necks encircled with chains of gold, were brought in. Edward now vowed by God and the swans that he would at once set out to Scotland, and avenge the wrongs done to Holy Church and the realm by the rebellious murderers of John Comyn. When Bruce was subdued, the king pledged himself that he would no more bear arms against Christian men, but would go to the Holy Land and die fighting against the infidel. The prince and the other new knights took the same vow, and the musters were ordered to assemble early in July at Carlisle. Thither the Prince of Wales was at once sent. Edward followed his son as quickly as his infirmities would allow.

On Michaelmas day Edward reached the Austin priory of Lanercost, near Carlisle. Here he took up his quarters for more than half a year, as the state of his health and his business with the pope combined to make it impossible for him to take the field in person. But the heavy hand of his generals was laid upon Scotland, and the new King Robert was soon reduced to such straits that he fled to the Western Isles for refuge, while the stern resolve of the old king to have done with clemency involved the unhappy Scots in worse desolation and destruction than ever. Many Scottish nobles were taken prisoners, and at once put to death as traitors. Their lands were confiscated and handed over to English earls in Edward's confidence. Bruce's own domains were overrun. Carrick was bestowed on Henry Percy; Annandale went to the young Earl of Hereford; another son-in-law of the king had the great earldom of Athol. This time Scotland was to be held by chains of iron in the merest and barest slavery. Yet even in his worst moods Edward bade his soldiers spare the common folk, whose only crime was obedience to the orders of their natural lords. He sternly rebuked the Prince of Wales for his indulgence in an indiscriminate slaughter that distinguished neither leader from follower, nor grown man from woman and child.

Edward suffered much from sickness during his stay at Lanercost, but he still found energy enough to move, in March 1307, to Carlisle to meet the parliament which he had summoned to assemble in the border city. With the return of summer, bad news again came from the seat of war. Bruce returned from his hiding-place, and the good-will of the mass of the population again allowed him to make headway against the strong armies of Edward. As soon as parliament was over, the old king resolved to take the field in person. He offered up in the cathedral church the horse-litter which had conveyed him from the south, and again mounted his charger and put himself at the head of the army that was pouring into Scotland. But his great spirit was no longer able to control his failing body. For two successive days he struggled on; but each day he could only manage to ride two miles, and on the third day he was forced to rest altogether. On the fourth day Edward managed to reach Burgh-on-Sands, a village less than six miles from Carlisle. He was now attacked by dysentery, and sank rapidly. As he lay dying he sent his last words of counsel to his absent son. He urged him to persevere in the subjection of Scotland, and to avoid unworthy favourites. His last thoughts turned to the two great enterprises on which he had bent his mind—the subjection of Scotland and the recovery of the Holy Land. Even after his death he longed to share in those great works. He begged his son to carry his bones about with him in his Scottish campaigns, so that even the dead Edward might still lead his warriors to victory against the hated enemy. He also requested that his heart should be sent to the Holy Land with a train of a hundred knights to fight for the recovery of the Sepulchre of the Lord. He then prepared himself for death, and, with a prayer for the divine mercy on his lips, quietly passed away on 7th July 1307, at the age of sixty-eight. With the great king died his great work, and the tragedy of his end was made more pitiful by the wretched farce of the reign of Edward II. His dying wishes were set at nought. The Scots campaign was given up. His body was sent with scanty reverence to an immediate burial-place at Westminster, where it now reposes under a plain monument of gray marble, but little corresponding to his greatness as a king, and upon which has been inscribed

"EDWARDUS PRIMUS SCOTORUM MALLEUS HIC EST. PACTUM SERVA."

But it was not only by reason of his son's unworthiness that Edward's most cherished plans were doomed to failure. He had attempted more than even his strong purpose could have successfully accomplished. But if an independent Scotland bore witness that Edward's greatest ambition was a failure, his work lived on in his own realm of England, where after-ages agreed to recognise in him one of the greatest and wisest of her rulers, and where the whole subsequent history of the land he loved so well bore daily witness to the strength and endurance of the great king's work.

THE END.

Printed in Great Britain
by Amazon

17600629R00132

165· 30·